Historical and Geneological Record.

J. H. Buffords Lith.

THE OLD HOUSE.

See page 143

A

HISTORICAL AND GENEOLOGICAL

RECORD

OF THE

DESCENDANTS OF

TIMOTHY ROCKWOOD.

BORN IN MEDWAY, JULY 5, 1727.
DIED IN HOLLISTON, FEB. 21, 1806.

COMPILED FROM AUTHENTIC SOURCES.

BY. E. L. ROCKWOOD.

"Children's children *are* the crown of old men ; and the glory of children *are* their fathers."—PROV. 17: 6.

BOSTON, MASS.,
PUBLISHED BY THE COMPILER.
1856.

Printed by Bazin & Chandler,
37 Cornhill, Boston.

TO THE

DESCENDANTS OF

TIMOTHY ROCKWOOD,

MY GRANDFATHER'S POSTERITY,

WHO ARE NOW SCATTERED AFAR, BUT WHOM

WE HOPE TO MEET IN

AN ETERNAL HOME WITH THE WHOLE

FAMILY IN HEAVEN.

THESE PAGES ARE

RESPECTFULLY DEDICATED BY

THEIR FRIEND,

THE COMPILER.

PREFACE.

ONE ignorant of his Parentage, would be justified in any degree of curiosity to discover it. But why stop at parents? Why not follow the line still farther back, and stop only when compeled to do so? It wonld seem a natural and reasonable curiosity, which thus gathers up the *names* of past generations, while a filial reverence would embalm the memory of the good among them.

We owe something to the future also. We have now the means of collecting names and dates, which, in a few years, those who might desire to do so, will not have. It seems wrong to let an opportunity pass which others coming after might thank us for improving.

The following Record was commenced in 1834, and, having been brought down to the present time — a desire expressed on the part of many to possess a copy, is the inducement to give it the permanence of a printed form. It is believed to be accurate and reliable. The sketches of character, and incidents of life introduced, give it variety, and it is hoped add to its value.

Thanks are due to those who have so freely and promptly furnished the informaiion requisite for its completion.

THE COMPILER.

Holliston, December, 1855.

RECORD.

Samuel Rockwood, the father of Timothy Rockwood, whose genealogy is the subject of these pages, was born in Medfield, Mass., April 15th, 1695, and died in Medway, Jan'y 11th, 1754. *

The Rockwoods, during the last part of the Sixteenth and the first of the Seventeenth Centuries, were called Rockets. Their names were pronounced Rocket and written Rocket in the old records. This Samuel was born a Rocket, lived a Rocket, but died a Rockwood. There is no evidence, however, that *their own signatures* were ever written any other way than Rockwood.

A large part of the town of Medway was taken from Medfield, and was not incorporated when this Samuel

* The names of the father and mother of this Samuel, were John Rocket and Bethia. They lived in Medfield. Was this the house of three generations? See Medfield Town Records.

was born. It is supposed that he never moved from the place of his birth, but that in this same place, he was born, lived a life of nearly three-score years, reared his family and died. Certain it is, that the birth-place of most of *his children* is now positively known. In 1713, when Medway was incorporated, this homestead of Samuel and birth-place of his children became a part of that town.

Again, in 1828, this part of Medway was set off, and became a part of Holliston. The *very spot* where the family mansion of this Puritanic Samuel stood, can now be identified, and pointed out to the passing traveller. It is in the east part of Holliston, on the Medway village road, on land of Mr. John Smith, a few rods east of his house. The old cellar is still plain to be seen, though now considerably filled up by the washing in of surrounding earth. *His descendants should not forget the spot.*

FIRST GENERATION.

CHILDREN OF SAMUEL ROCKWOOD.

SAMUEL ROCKWOOD, the father of TIMOTHY ROCKWOOD, was born in Medfield, April 15th, 1695 — died in Medway, Jan'y 11th, 1754. He had 2 wives—Mary and Sarah — and 7 children, namely:

Samuel Rockwood, jr., born May 3, 1724.	
TIMOTHY ROCKWOOD, *was born in Medway, July* 5, 1724.	
Moses Rockwood,	born May 19, 1737.
Aaron "	born March 5, 1744.
Amos "	born July 20, 1751.
Samuel " jr.,	born Nov. 3, 1752.
Mary "	born March 2, 1754.

SECOND GENERATION.

CHILDREN OF TIMOTHY ROCKWOOD.

Timothy Rockwood, was born July 5, 1727. Lived in Holliston. Died Feb. 21, 1806.

He had 4 wives, 12 children, 47 grand-children, 157 great grand-children, 196 great, great grand-children, and 43 great, great, great grand children — of whom 1 child, 16 grand-children, 101 great grand-children, 170 great, great grand-children, and 35 great, great, great grand-children are now living.

His whole number of decendants are four hundred and fifty-five.

TIMOTHY ROCKWOOD,

Married Elizabeth Perry, Jan. 24, 1750.

1. Timothy Rockwood, jr., born Oct. 14, 1751.
2. Elizabeth " born Dec. 23, 1753.
3. Samuel " born 1755 — died 1758.
4. Deborah " born Dec. 10, 1758.
5. Samuel " born 1760 — died 1760.
6. Rhoda " born Oct. 12, 1763.

Elizabeth P., wife of Timothy Rockwood, died Nov. 1765.
Timothy Rockwood, married Jemima Underwood, 1767.
Jemima U., wife of Timothy Rockwood, died 1768.
Timothy Rockwood, married Alice Littlefield, Aug 22, 1771.

7. Aaron Rockwood, born July 6, 1772 — died 1779.
8. Mariam " born Dec. 13, 1773—died 1785.
9. Lucretia " born July 25, 1775.
10. Ann " born June 14, 1777.
11. Luther " born Jan'y 7, 1780.
12. Calvin " born Dec. 24, 1783 — died 1785.

Alice L., wife of Timothy Rockwood, died Jan'y 1784.
Timothy Rockwood, married Deborah Fairbanks, Mar. 1787.
Deborah F., wife of Timothy Rockwood, died May 21, 1805.

At the time, or very soon after the marriage of Timothy Rockwood in 1750, he moved from the home of his father Samuel, and settled a short distance west of Holliston centre. A part of the original homestead is now occupied by his only surviving son and child, Luther Rockwood.

He was a large owner of real estate, both in Holliston and elsewhere. He was an ardent and abiding supporter of the cause of liberty in the great struggle for American Independence — a firm and reliable friend of the widow and the fatherless, in those times which tried men's souls. He sustained almost every office in the gift of the town, peculiar to the precarious times of the Revolution; — was one of the committee "*to paste up the names of all those who sold, or consumed any of the East India Teas.*" During several successive years he was one of the committee "*to hire soldiers to go into the army.*" The General Court required the inhabitants of the several towns to furnish our army with a quantity of beef and clothing, "Granted 100 and 30 pound hard money to purchase beef for the town of Holliston." Timothy Rockwood was one of the committee "To procure beef and pay money in lieu thereof, agreeable to the resolves of the General Court." He was one of the committee "*To inspect the inhabitants of the town and learn the opinions of each person in relation to the acts of the Provincial Congress.*" In 1776, the town "voted to choose a committee to draw up some instrument for the representatives of this town, relative to forming a Constitution for this State." — Agreeable to the resolves of the General Court, Timothy Rockwood was one of the committee.

Though it may seem somewhat out of place here, yet

we venture to insert two short extracts from the Records of the Town of Holliston, to show the spirit and temper of the *men* who lived and *acted* through the trying times in which our honored and venerated progenitor was so conspicuous.

In 1775, the town Voted — "That no man shall serve in any town office, or in any place, where he shall refuse, or neglect to subscribe his consent to, and compliance with, the advice and association of the last Continental Congress, and that such person shall be treated with neglect."

It was also, the same year, Voted — "Not to choose into office, or employ in any business of the town, any person that has appeared an enemy to this country in their present struggle with Great Britain." *

The following sketch of the life and character of Timothy Rockwood, prepared by Rev. Timothy Dickenson of Holliston, a venerable father in the ministry, is here inserted. It is a true copy of the original in the possession of his only surviving son, Luther Rockwood.

Died, at Holliston, Feb. 21, 1806, Mr. Timothy Rockwood, aged 78.

The following were some of the Traits which distinguished his character. Such was the situation of his youth, that he had no opportunity to acquire what is now considered a common school education. He rose into notice in the circle of

* For further information, see Holliston Town Records.

his acquaintance by the energies of his own mind. Such was the power of his Memory, that in all his extensive concerns he needed not to keep Book-accounts; he was able to recollect past particulars in his Reckonings with such ease and accuracy, as gave satisfaction to the many with whom he had dealings. He loved husbandry; and by the labor of his hands, by Judgment in affairs, by punctuality in business, and by integrity and uprightness in his dealings with mankind, he was blessed with large property. By precept and example he bore his pointed testimony against idleness and luxury. The poor ever acknowledged him their friend: his general method of helping them, was by his good counsel and by placing them in circumstances and situations to held themselves. His Counsel and Advice in cases of difficulty, ware much sought after and respected. The Town looked upon him as a father. Economy and hospitality were united under his peaceful roof.

He lived to follow Four tender and affectionate wives to the Grave, all of whom he married within sight of his own door; and what is worthy of remark, in all his connections he was peculiarly happy. His last wife he survived but nine months.

He was often in affliction, not only by the loss of his wives, but by the Death of many of his children and grand-children: under all these trials he expressed affectionate sensibility and composed resignation.

His Family connections are numerous and respectable; and a large proportion of the Town as mourning relations, followed his Remains to the Grave.

From early life he was a professor of the Christian Religion, and a regular attendant upon its institutions and ordinances.

The Town, in whose peace and prosperity he was devoutly interested, and the large circle of his connections, have just reason to respect the Memory of Mr. Rockwood.

Holliston, March 3, 1806.

He was interred in the old Central burying ground in Holliston.

The following is the inscription on the monument erected to his memory:

IN MEMORY OF

MR. TIMOTHY ROCKWOOD,

WHO DIED IN FEB. 22, 1806.

IN THE 79TH YEAR

OF HIS AGE.

He was pious and devout, and eminently useful in Society. A numerous race of Descendants, will long bedew his grave with their tears.

THIRD GENERATION.

CHILDREN OF TIMOTHY ROCKWOOD,

AND FIRST CHILD OF TIMOTHY ROCKWOOD, BORN IN 1727.

TIMOTHY ROCKWOOD was born Oct. 14, 1751. Lived in Holliston. Died Feb. 19, 1831.

He had 10 children, 58 grand-children, 119 great grand-children, and 34 great, great grand-children, of whom 1 child, 38 grand-children, 97 great grand-children, and 25 great, great grand-children are now living.

Timothy Rockwood married Margaret Parker, 1770.

1.	Nathan Rockwood,	born May 8, 1771.	
2.	Elizabeth	"	" Apr. 10, 1773—died Sep. 3, 1775.
3.	Nahum	"	born Oct. 8, 1775.
4.	William	"	born Nov. 13, 1777.
5.	Aaron	"	born Oct. 28, 1779.
6.	Sophia	"	born Oct. 12, 1782.
7.	Ezra	"	born Nov. 5, 1784.
8.	Millie	"	born Dec. 26, 1786.
9.	Timothy	"	born Jan. 17, 1789.
10.	Calvin	"	born June 3, 1792.

The following Obituary of Timothy Rockwood, is copied from the *Boston Recorder*, of Feb. 22, 1831:

DIED, in Holliston, Mass., Feb. 19, 1831, Mr. Timothy Rockwood, aged 79.

The decendants of the deceased number as follows:—10 children, of whom 8 are now living; grand-children 59, of whom 9 are deceased; great grand-children 26, of whom 1 is dead. The whole number is 95; and the whole number living is 83. The deceased was highly respected in life for the many amiable traits of character which he possessed—was eminently distinguished as a *peace-maker*, himself a pattern of kindness and gentleness, was honored by his towns-men with most of the offices in their gift, and was twice elected representative to the General Court. He has left behind a good name, which is better than precious ointment, and a large circle of relatives and friends to whom his memory will be dear.

FOURTH GENERATION.

CHILDREN OF NATHAN ROCKWOOD.

NATHAN ROCKWOOD, born May 8, 1771. Lived in Hopkinton. Died Aug. 7, 1841. Married Joanna Day, 1794.

Deborah Rockwood,	born Sep. 26, 1795.
Dexter "	born Dec. 5, 1797.
Betsey "	born June 13, 1800.
Ezekiel Day "	born Feb. 23, 1802.
Joanna " "	born July 23, 1804.

Joanna D. wife of Nathan Rockwood, died Oct. 25, 1804.
Nathan Rockwood, married Olive McFarland, Nov. 10, 1805.

Nathan Rockwood, jr., born Sep. 14, 1806—died Sep. 16, 1851.
Emily Augusta Rockwood, born Mar. 30, 1808.
Sophia Rockwood, born May 21, 1810.
Charlotte " born May 12, 1812.
Fanny Wares " born July 9, 1814—died Oct. 4, 1852.
Olive " born May 23, 1816.
Lucretia " born June 17, 1819.

Nathan Rockwood was the first born of the third generation. He lived in the town of his nativity until 1794. He then located permanently in Hopkinton. He could not say, as did the sons of Jacob, " thy servants are 12 brethren, the sons of one man ; " but could say, we are 10 brethren, and of my children there were 12.

A remarkable fact relative to his family is, that all grew up to manhood, and were permitted to enjoy each other's society for almost thirty years.

He was interred at the Central Cemetery in Hopkinton, and was followed to the grave by a large assemblage of mourners. On his tombstone is inscribed—" Blessed are they that hunger and thirst after righteousness."

The following original lines were dedicated to Olive, the second wife of Nathan Rockwood, who died Oct. 22, 1842: —

They have laid thee in thy grave, mother,
  My heart is full of woe,
I cannot still its mournings,
  How can I let thee go?
How dark the future seems, mother,
  To thy poor sorrowing child,
The thought that I am motherless
  Hath well-nigh made me wild.

They say I should be glad, mother,
  That thy toilsome journey's o'er —
Be glad! when I remember
  I shall see thy face no more!
They never knew thee here, mother,
  Nor what thou wast to me;
The light of life is darkened,
  " 'T is best it so should be."

When I would be glad for thee, mother,
  The bitter thought will come,
That I have none to love me now —
  That I have no earthly home.
I shall find no other friend, mother,
  Through all life's weary way,
That will love me so unselfishly,
  Or for me, like thee, pray.

I hear thy gentle voice, mother,
  In calm, sweet words of peace:
Thou art chiding thy erring child, mother,
  And bidding her murmurs cease.

I will, I will, if I can, dear mother,
  Be glad thou hast gone home;
Like thee, may I be waiting
  When the call for me shall come.

Thou hast not forgotten thy child, mother,
  Oft I feel thy presence near,
Whispering words of hope and love
  Into my listening ear.
I thank thee, blessed Saviour,
  For the hope that thou hast given,—
If I live aright on earth,
  We yet shall meet in heaven.

FIFTH GENERATION.

CHILDREN OF DEBORAH ROCKWOOD.

Deborah Rockwood, born Sept. 26, 1795. Lives in Hopkinton. Married Lawson McFarland in 1814.

Thomas McFarland,	born Apr. 24, 1814.	
Cromwell G.	"	born Feb. 7, 1819.
Emily A.	"	born Jan. 7, 1823.
Wallace	"	born Feb. 1, 1825.
Charles B.	"	born Mar. 7, 1832--died Apr. 25, 1834.
Charles	"	born Sep. 8, 1834.
Eliza R.	"	born May 17, 1836.
Jane	"	born Apr. 7, 1838—died Apr. 10, 1839.

Lawson McFarland, the husband of Deborah Rockwood above mentioned, was thrown from his carriage by his horse taking fright. He was so much injured, that he survived the accident but a few hours. He died in the fall of 1853.

SIXTH GENERATION.

CHILDREN OF CROMWELL McFARLAND.

Cromwell McFarland, born Feb. 7, 1819. Lives in Hopkinton. Married Hannah Phipps, June 2, 1842.

Curtis McFarland,	born June 10, 1844.
Anna "	born July 3, 1850.
Henry "	born Dec., 17, 1852.

CHILDREN OF EMILY A. M'FARLAND.

Emily A. McFarland, born Jan. 7, 1823. Lives in West Boylston. Married Thomas Phelps, Jan 4, 1846.

Effee Jane Phelps, born May 23, 1853.

CHILDREN OF WALLACE M'FARLAND.

Wallace McFarland, born Feb. 1, 1825. Lives in Hopkinton. Married Julia Fletcher, Feb. 8, 1844.

Ida McFarland,	born Nov. 22, 1847.
Emily "	born Feb. 22, 1850.
Thomas "	born Sept. 22, 1853.

CHILDREN OF ELIZA R. M'FARLAND.

Eliza R. McFarland, born May 17, 1836. Lives in Portsmouth, Maine. Married John Berry, July 2, 1850.

Henry Berry,	born Jan. 17, 1851.
Eliza Jane Berry,	born July 4, 1853.

FIFTH GENERATION.

CHILDREN OF DEXTER ROCKWOOD.

Dexter Rockwood, born Dec. 5, 1797. Lives in Ashland. Married Elizabeth L. Eames, Jan. 1, 1822.

Julia Ann Rockwood, born Dec. 13, 1822.
Albert " born Sep. 18 1824—died Mar. 22, 1851.
Henry Clay " born Feb. 15, 1828.

Dexter Rockwood is a Deacon of the Congregational Church in Ashland, under the pastoral care of Rev. Wm. M. Thayer — an office indicative of morality and unfeigned love to the cause of Christ.

TESTIMONIAL TO THE LIFE AND CHARACTER OF ALBERT ROCKWOOD, BY REV. WM. M. THAYER.

Albert Rockwood was the son of Dea. Dexter and Mrs. Elizabeth L. Rockwood of Ashland, Mass. He was a young man of marked character. Possessing more than ordinary intellectual powers, and being disposed to make the best use of his attainments, and more than all being a consistent follower of Christ, he was abundantly prepared to make his mark upon the world. But God cut him down in the midst of his days. For many months he suffered extremely with an abscess which baffled medical skill. He bore his sufferings with that fortitude and submission for which the true Christian is always distinguished. His death was emphatically that of the righteous, and his departure made an irreparable breach in the circle from which he was removed.

SIXTH GENERATION.

CHILDREN OF JULIA ANN ROCKWOOD.

Julia Ann Rockwood, born Dec. 13, 1822. Lives in Milford. Married David Brewer, May 30, 1848.

Fred. Brewer,	born Feb. 15, 1849.
Alyn "	born June 13, 1851.

FIFTH GENERATION.

CHILDREN OF BETSEY ROCKWOOD.

Betsey Rockwood, born June 13, 1800. Lives in Hopkinton. Married Thomas Barber in 1818.

Joanna Day	Barber,	born Aug. 18, 1819.
Curtis H.	"	born July 23, 1821.
John	"	born Jan. 3, 1823.
Albert	"	born July 11, 1824.
Charles	"	born May 26, 1825–died Dec. 27, '30.
George	"	born July 17, 1827.
Thomas jr.	"	born May 20, 1829—died July 4, '49.
Emily Elizabeth	"	born Jan. 1, 1831.
Charles H.	"	born Nov. 18, 1832.
Edward Everett	"	born Jan. 15, 1837.
Sarah Jane	"	born June 17, 1839.
Mary Ann	"	born Sept. 30, 1841.
William Henry	"	born Oct. 17, 1843.

Thomas Barber, husband and father of the above, died in 1852.

The circumstances attending the death of Thomas Barber, jr., are peculiarly melancholy, and afflicting. He was drowned in North Pond, Hopkinton, July 4, 1849. He went out on the morning of this our country's holiday, in company with five others on a fishing excursion, which pastime he had for a long time anticipated. They had taken dinner on a small island a short distance out from the shore. While on their return, Thomas thought he would *try* to swim. He was no swimmer, and was very soon seen drowning. His companions used their utmost efforts to save his life, and all hazarded their own in the attempt. Alas! their efforts were unavailing. He had gone down to the dead. Almost the last words he uttered were, "we shall have a good time." His body was brought home about sunset.

This close of the nation's holiday was, to this family and their friends, one of mourning and lamentation. Verily "we know not what a day may bring forth."

The following testimony to the character of Thomas Barber, jr., from the pen of Rev. J. C. Webster, of Hopkinton, is here introduced. It was kindly furnished the compiler by J. A. Woolson, Esq., of Boston, near friend of our deceased relative: —

The memory of Thomas Barber, jr., is fragrant with pleasing recollections. He possessed, in a high degree, a naturally kind and amiable disposition. He was an affectionate son and brother, and a general favorite with all who knew him. The immediate impression which he made upon other minds was happy, and it increased upon acquaintance. He was open, frank, guileless. He was always ready to oblige others, and even to anticipate their wants. This trait in his character was very noticeable by those who traded with him. It rendered him valuable to his employers. Had he lived, it would have been a good capital for him in business. His countenance was always lighted up with a pleasant smile and a genial fellow feeling, which seemed to say, "what shall I do for you?"

He never, in so many words, expressed a personal interest in religion. But he was never known to treat it lightly, and all his conduct indicated a high regard for it. He was an habitual attendant upon public worship. And he was a member of the Sabbath School where some other young men of his own age were apt to feel that they were too old. In short, he was one of those young persons whom we expect, the older they grow, to exhibit a character of great moral purity. And his friends were not left without reason to hope that he might already have had that spiritual germ implanted in his heart, which would eventually have developed itself, had his life been spared, in a mature Christian experience.

The general esteem in which he was held was signally manifested by the universal grief produced by his death, and the large concourse of citizens of all ranks and ages at his funeral. And the affection of his more intimate companions, who were enjoying a day of innocent recreation with him when he came to his untimely end, is exhibited by a beautiful marble obelisk, which they reared upon the spot where his mortal remains were laid.

SIXTH GENERATION.

CHILDREN OF JOANNA D. BARBER.

JOANNA D. BARBER, born Aug. 18, 1819. Lives in Hopkinton. Married E. A. Bates, Jan. 7, 1841.

Theodore Sedgwick Bates, born March 24, 1845.
Ella Jane Bates, born Apr. 1, 1850—died Feb. 8, '52.
Jennie Sabea " born April 2, 1853.
Thomas Barber " born Feb. 3, 1855.

CHILDREN OF CURTIS H. BARBER.

Curtis H. Barber, born July 23, 1821. Lives in Boston. Married Julia Forbes, Dec. 1842.

A son, born May 1844—died May 1844.
Twins, born 1846—died 1846.

Julia F., wife of Curtis H. Barber, died January 1846.
Curtis H. Barber, married Olivia A. Eames, 1847.

Frances Barber, born Sept. 1847—died Jan. '48.
Thomas " born Dec. 1849.
Frank " born Dee. 1853—died Oct. '54.

FIFTH GENERATION.

GEORGE BARBER, born July 17, 1827. Lives in Hopkinton. Married Susan B. Osborn, Nov. 15, 1853.

EMILY E. BARBER, born Jan. 1, 1831. Lives in Hopkinton. Married Homer Gibbs, May 3, 1854.

CHILDREN OF EZEKIEL DAY ROCKWOOD.

Ezekiel Day Rockwood, born Feb. 23, 1802. Lives in Southboro'. Married Ann S. Williams, April 1828.

Charles Henry Rockwood,		born April 13, 1829.
Alfred Elliot	"	born April 28, 1833.
Edward Payson	"	born Aug. 7, 1835.
Justin Edwards	"	born Oct. 5, 1839.

Ezekiel Day Rockwood, in youth and early manhood experienced many of the trials of life. Its shady side was emphatically his. But the tide of his affairs seem now to have turned, and all bespeaks prosperity. He has wealth, honor, contentment and godliness, which is great gain. Moreover he possesses the virtues of benevolence and hospitality.

FOURTH GENERATION.

JOANNA D. ROCKWOOD, born July 23, 1804. Lives in Holliston. Married Horatia N. Johnson, April 1832.

FIFTH GENERATION.

CHILDREN OF NATHAN F. ROCKWOOD.

NATHAN F. ROCKWOOD, born Sept. 14, 1806. Lived in New York City. Married Lucretia Cox, July 28, 1841. Died Sept. 16, 1851.

Mary Louisa Rockwood,		born June 23, 1842.
Emma Frances	"	born Jan. 3, 1844.
Ida Olive	"	born Nov. 26, 1845.
Adelaide Sophia	"	born Oct. 18, 1847.
Charles Edgar	"	born Jan. 11, 1850.

The tolling of the bell, occasioned by the death of Nathan F. Rockwood, cast an unwonted gloom over surviving brothers and sisters. By his removal his widow was left to mourn the loss of a kind and confiding partner, and his children, a good father. The community also feel his loss, for he was a valuable citizen. He was emphatically a friend to the poor and to those who were laboring under pecuniary embarrassment. He had an active and benevolent spirit, and verily "cast his bread upon the waters," and the promise annexed is being verified to his mourning widow. During his sickness he looked forward to death with composed resignation.

We trust the day of his dissolution found him in the mansions of the blest in heaven.

"There is a calm for those who weep
A rest for weary pilgrims found;
And while the mouldering ashes sleep
Low in the ground;

"The soul of origin divine,
God's glorious image freed from clay,
In heaven's eternal sphere shall shine,
A star of day!"

☞ For family of EMILY R. JONES, see page 146.

FIFTH GENERATION.

CHILDREN OF SOPHIA ROCKWOOD.

Sophia Rockwood born May 21, 1810. Lives in Worcester. Married Charles Ager, 1833.

Charles Ager, jr., born March 28, 1834.
Lizzie Nelson Ager, born Nov. 1, 1849.

FOURTH GENERATION.

Charlotte Rockwood, born May 12, 1812. Lives in Hopkinton. Married William Bemis, Dec. 22, 1852.

FIFTH GENERATION.

CHILDREN OF FANNY W. ROCKWOOD.

Fanny W. Rockwood, born July 9, 1814. Lived in Worcester. Married Henry Fairbanks, May 17, 1836. Died Oct. 4, 1853.

Frederick Agustin Fairbanks, born Apr. 10, 1838—died May 1, 1844.
Helen Fairbanks, born Aug. 16, 1839—died Apr. 19, '44.
Caroline Louisa " born Aug. 16, 1839—died Nov. 5, '39.
Herbert Henry " born March 23, 1847.
Frederick Walter " born Jan. 31, 1850.

We trust Mrs. Fairbanks died the death of a Christian. It is delightful to contemplate a departed spirit when we are assured that it is in heavenly mansions in company with Christ and his chosen ones. "Death does not cancel the great bond that holds commingling spirits." This consideration should lift us above earthly things, and aid us to walk softly before God.

Bunyan has described the Christian pilgrimage of our departed relative. The Parchment Roll was her lamp and light, though she was not unfrequently impeded in her course by Apolyon and his legion. When she was crossing the deep river of death, the promise of Christ was verified to her: "When thou passest through the waters I will be with thee, and through the rivers they shall not overflow thee." Her last words were, "peace, peace."

FOURTH GENERATION.

CHILDREN OF NAHUM ROCKWOOD.

Nahum Rockwood, born Oct. 8, 1775. Lived in Leicester. Married Elizabeth Newton, April 3, 1799. Died Dec. 26, 1853.

Mary Rockwood, born Apr. 12, 1801--died Aug. 1, 1854.
Ursula Cutler Rockwood, born Jan. 16, 1804.
Elizabeth Newton " born Nov. 11, 1807.
Timothy Parker " born Jan. 19, 1812.
Milton " born Oct. 14, 1819.

Nahum Rockwood became a resident of Leicester about the year 1800. I have learned but a single incident of his life, prior to 1810. It was related to me by one of his brothers, who has since gone home to his rest in heaven. On a certain occasion *he heaped his corn to save toll when he measured it for the miller*, and this so tormented him, that it was the means of his conversion.

The following testimonial to Nahum Rockwood, dated July 13, 1855, was cheerfully given to his relatives by John Nelson, D.D., whose intercourse with the deceased was intimate and cordial for a period of more than forty years: —

DEA. NAHUM ROCKWOOD, died in Leicester Dec. 26, 1853, aged 78 years, 4 months and 18 days. He was a thriving and active farmer, always industrious and always the friend of good order. He was much respected as a neighbor and citizen. His integrity in every situation was unimpeached. He had the confidence of all. In his own affairs and in the affairs of the public, so far as he was concerned in them, he was remarkably intent on having everything done right and done promptly. He was received as a member of the church November 5, 1810, and was chosen as one of the deacons in April of the next year, 1811. This office in the church he sustained with much fidelity till the close of life; was also appointed to many important and honorable town offices — all of which, he *well* and *faithfully* sustained. In his family, as a husband and father, he was provident, kind and exemplary. As a Christian, Dea. Rockwood was sound in faith and devoted. He had warmth of feeling and zeal in promoting the cause of Christ. "Blessed are the dead that die in the Lord."

Mary, the daughter of Nahum Rockwood, was peculiarly tender and sympathetic in her feelings. Many a weary hour has she spent by the bedside of the sick, always ready to lend a helping hand to those that were in affliction. She gathered around her a large circle of friends, who greatly loved her while she lived, and greatly lamented her death. Her last sickness was severe and protracted, which she bore with Christian patience and resignation. During several weeks previous to her departure, it seemed to her friends that death had lost its sting, and that she had already commenced her entrance upon the blissful realities of a better world. When the last hour *did* come, she peacefully took leave of her friends, to be with earth and earthly things no more forever.

> "She died at twilight — at the close
> Of a bright summer's day,
> As nature sunk in calm repose,
> Her spirit passed away.
>
> "At twilight — as the earth shut out
> The sun's last lingering ray,
> Her spirit bathed in heavenly light
> Passed joyously away."

FIFTH GENERATION.

CHILDREN OF URSULA C. ROCKWOOD.

Ursula C. Rockwood, born Jan. 16, 1804. Lived in Leicester. Married Edwin Waite, 1825. Died May 21, 1838.

Mary Emeline Waite,	born Sep. 12, 1828.
Phebe Whittemore "	born April 27, 1832.

CHILD OF ELIZABETH N. ROCKWOOD.

Elizabeth N. Rockwood, born Nov. 11, 1807. Lives in Leicester. Married Elijah Harkness, 1827.

Emma Agustin Harkness, born Jan. 8, 1845—died Jan. 8, 1847.

CHILDREN OF TIMOTHY P. ROCKWOOD.

Timothy P. Rockword, born Jan. 19, 1812. Lived in Leicester. Married Rebecca Draper, May 3, 1836. Died Sept. 2, 1851.

Cornelia Elizabeth Rockwood,		born April 12, 1838.
Edward Payson	"	born Oct. 28, 1840.
Mary Eliza	"	born Dec. 26, 1846.
Louisa Maria	"	born March 16, 1850.

Timothy P. Rockwood died the death of the Christian, much lamented by all who knew him.

CHILD OF MILTON ROCKWOOD.

Milton Rockwood, born Oct. 14, 1819. Lives in Leicester. Married Susan Elliot, June 5, 1843.

Edwin Waite Rockwood, born June 8, 1848.

FOURTH GENERATION.

CHILDREN OF WILLIAM ROCKWOOD.

William Rockwood, born Nov. 13, 1777. Lived in Holliston. Married Mary Burnap, March 31, 1803. Died March 7, 1848.

William Eaton Rockwood,	born March 11, 1807.
Mary Morse "	born March 25, 1811.

Col. William Rockwood was the third son of Timothy Rockwood. Resided in Holliston until 1809, then removed to Hopkinton, where he lived 9 years. While there, was much in the service of the town, discharging the duties of many of its principal offices.

In 1818, he returned to Holliston, and located himself upon the homestead of his father, Timothy, which joined the school-house in district number two. He possessed, in a large degree, disinterestedness and kindliness of character. Thelatter trait being prominently exemplified towards the school-children of the district, who, in term-time, one would be more than half ready to conclude he had adopted as his own. This course he pursued till the close of life. Members of school district number two in his day, will long revere his memory. He was a strenuous advocate of most of the educational, social, and political reforms of the day. He remembered the poor. They ever found in him a friend—good advice and "material aid" being wisely blended.

The Hollistonians loved and respected him—he was elected by them to officiate in many responsible and trustworthy offices, from 1820 to 1840. He also took much interest in military affairs, which was a high honor in his day.

Upon his tombstone are the following words: "*Blessed is he that considereth the poor, the Lord will deliver him in time of trouble.*"

FIFTH GENERATION.

CHILDREN OF WM. E. ROCKWOOD.

William E. Rockwood, born March 11, 1807. Lived in Holliston. Married Elizabeth Daniels, May 16, 1833. Died June 15, 1836.

Edward Everett	Rockwood,	born June 1834.
Mary Elizabeth	"	died June 22, 1836.
Edward Everett	"	died Oct. 2, 1855.

William E. Rockwood died of lingering consumption, aged 29.

CHILD OF MARY M. ROCKWOOD.

Mary M. Rockwood, born March 25, 1811. Lives in Holliston. Married John Fisk, May 11, 1831.

Elbridge Burnap Fisk, born Oct. 28, 1832—died June 9, 1843, aged 10 years and 7 months.

Mr. and Mrs. Fisk are active and exemplary members of the Methodist Church. They have an adopted son, John Noble York Fisk, born Jan. 13, 1846.

FOURTH GENERATION.

CHILDREN OF AARON ROCKWOOD.

Aaron Rockwood, born Oct. 28, 1779. Married Milly Watkins, 1801. Died Aug. 9, 1827.

Newell	Rockwood,	born July 11, 1801.
Mary Ann	"	born Feb. 8, 1805.
Aaron Watkins	"	born May 2, 1807.
Caroline	"	born Feb. 8, 1810—died Mar. 16, 1824.
Milly Parker	"	born Aug. 4, 1812—died July 9, 1824.
Ezra Brown	"	born Dec. 29, 1816.
Harriet Atwood	"	born May 25, 1821.
Sabrina Morse	"	born March 25, 1823.

Aaron Rockwood, soon after marriage, located in Medway. Subsequently he lived in Bellingham and Franklin. When in Medway he was somewhat active in town and military duties. Prior to his death he lived in Hopkinton, where he died.

Milly W., wife of Aaron Rockwood, died in Holliston, Aug. 22, 1841. Their graves, together with two of their children, are to be found in a remote part of the old Cemetery at West Medway.

FIFTH GENERATION.

CHILDREN OF NEWELL ROCKWOOD.

Newell Rockwood, born July 11, 1801. Lives in Holliston. Married Ann S. Winter, April 20, 1823.

Ann S. Rockwood, died August, 1824.

Newell Rockwood, married Sukey Leland, March, 12, 1826.

Ann Sophia Rockwood,	born Dec. 10, 1827.
George Leland "	born Dec. 9, 1829.

Sukey L., wife of Newell Rockwood, died Dec. 28, 1829.

Newell Rockwood, married Sarah Smith, Oct. 6, 1830.

Sarah Jemima Rockwood, born Oct. 17, 1831, died Nov. 24 '33.

SIXTH GENERATION.

CHILD OF ANNE S. ROCKWOOD.

Anne S. Rockwood, born Dec. 10, 1827. Married George F. Smith, 1845.

Martha Jane Smith, born 1845—died May, 1846.

George F. Smith, died Aug., 1846.

FIFTH GENERATION.

ANNE S. SMITH.

Anne S. Smith, married Nathan H. Johnson, June, 1847.

Nathan H. Johnson, died Dec. 1851.

Anne S. Johnson, married Gilbert Lackey, Aug. 1854. Lives in Needham.

SIXTH GENERATION.

CHILD OF GEORGE L. ROCKWOOD.

George L. Rockwood, born Dec. 9, 1829. Lives in Westboro'. Married Amanda M. Johnson, Aug. 28, 1851.

Irene Gertrude Rockwood, born Oct. 22, 1853.

FIFTH GENERATION.

CHILDREN OF MARY ANN ROCKWOOD.

Mary Ann Rockwood, born Feb. 8, 1805. Lives in West Medway. Married Simeon Fisher, 1824.

Caroline Rockwood Fisher, born 1825.
George Simeon Fisher, born Sept. 1828.
Elias Thayer " born Aug. 13, 1835, died Mar. 8, '37.
Milly Ann " born Nov. 24, 1837.
Willard Pierce " born Oct. 2, 1842.

SIXTH GENERATION.

CHILDREN OF CAROLINE R. FISHER.

CAROLINE R. FISHER, born in 1825. Lived in Holliston. Married Mellen C. Bragg, Oct. 17, 1843. Died in Holliston, Sept. 12, 1849.

Elizabeth Caroline Bragg, born Aug. 19, 1844.
John Fisher Bragg, born Aug. 2, 1845.
Irene Parkhurst " born Aug. 22, 1846, died Sep. 22, 1849.

"Mrs. Bragg was an exemplary woman, an affectionate wife, and tender mother. Her absence is keenly felt in the domestic circle from which she was so suddenly removed. A large concourse of mourners followed her remains to their resting-place, after receiving the consolations of the gospel from the Rev. Dr. Ide, of Medway."

CHILDREN OF GEORGE S. FISHER.

GEORGE S. FISHER, born. Sept. 1828. Lives in Holliston. Married Mira A. Babcock, Nov. 22, 1852.

Abby Maria Fisher, born May 26, 1853.
Carrie Louise " born July 2, 1855.

FIFTH GENERATION.

CHILDREN OF AARON W. ROCKWOOD.

Aaron W. Rockwood, born May 2, 1807. Lives in Boston. Married Almira Cobb, April 1830.

Angeline Almira Rockwood,		born March, 1833.
Jane Matilda	"	born Sept. 14, 1840.

Aaron W. Rockwood has been keeper of a public house in Wrentham and Medway, and more subsequently in Boston, of the Old Lamb Tavern and Fountain House. He is of fearful temperament, and judges by the report of his family that his friends may think the Rockwood race on the decline. Hopes, however, that he shall be able to give the location of grand-chidren in the next number — a twig from the old stock.

FOURTH GENERATION.

Ezra B. Rockwood, born Dec. 29, 1816. Lives in Fitchburg. Married Hannah R. Sargent, Dec. 25, 1846.

Hannah R., wife of Ezra B. Rockwood, died of consumption in Fitchburg, March 15, 1854. She was interred at Orford, N. H., the place of her nativity.

Ezra B. Rockwood is a self-made man, and is in thriving circumstances.

FIFTH GENERATION.

CHILDREN OF HARRIET A. ROCKWOOD.

HARRIET A. ROCKWOOD, born May 25, 1821. Lives in Ashland. Married Addison Warfield, May 13, 1840.

Harriet Milly Warfield, born May 7, 1841, died June 28, 1841.
Elias Addison " born July 15, 1842, " Feb. 6, 1845.
Aaron Rockwood " born July 20, 1846.
Amanda Watkins, " born May 20, 1849.

FOURTH GENERATION.

SABRINA M. ROCKWOOD, born March 25, 1823. Lives in Holliston. Married Amory Cutler, Jan. 10, 1852.

FOURTH GENERATION.

CHILDREN OF SOPHIA ROCKWOOD.

SOPHIA ROCKWOOD, born Oct. 12, 1782. Lived in Holliston. Married Abner Holbrook, July 5, 1801. Died May 17, 1849.

Almira Holbrook, born Nov. 13, 1802.
Joanna " born July 11, 1805—died Feb. 26, 1809.

Abner Holbrook, died Dec. 2, 1806. Sophia R. Holbrook, married Martin Cutler, 1810.

Simeon Cutler,	born July 12, 1811.
Betsey Mellen Cutler,	born April 18, 1813.
Abner Holbrook "	born May 7, 1815.
Josephus Wheaton "	born Feb. 19, 1817.
Martin Luther "	born Oct. 16, 1819.
Timothy Rockwood "	born May 3, 1822.

Mrs. Cutler was industrious and enterprising. She united with the Congregational Church, in Holliston, in 1827, under the ministry of Rev. Charles Fitch.

FIFTH GENERATION.

CHILDREN OF ALMIRA HOLBROOK.

Almira Holbrook, born November 13, 1802. Lives in Holliston. Married Appleton Bridges, 1823.

Adeline Bridges,	born Dec. 30, 1823.
Alpheus Bridges	born Sep. 27, 1825.
Joanna Holbrook "	born Jan. 13, 1828—died June 14, 1847.
Clarissa Jane "	born May 22, 1830.
Mary Ann "	born May 4, 1832.
Appleton "	born Sep. 6, 1835—died Sep. 9, 1837.
Maranda Smith "	born Sep. 5, 1838.
Emeline Augusta "	born July 15, 1841.

Mr. Bridges has been an invalid nearly six years, besides, he is almost blind. Mrs. Bridges is provident and resolute — will do him good, and not evil all the days of her life.

SIXTH GENERATION.

CHILDREN OF ADELINE BRIDGES.

ADALINE BRIDGES, born Dec. 30, 1823. Lives in Holliston. Married Everett Smith, Dec. 8, 1844.

Albert Bridges Smith,	born Nov. 25, 1845.
Abby Joanna "	born May 14, 1851.

FIFTH GENERATION.

ALPHEUS BRIDGES.

ALPHEUS BRIDGES, born Sep. 27, 1825. Lives in Holliston. Married Adelia M. Bailey, Nov. 28, 1849.

SIXTH GENERATION.

CHILD OF CLARISSA J. BRIDGES.

CLARISSA J. BRIDGES, born, May 22, 1830. Lives in Hopkinton. Married Charles Watkins, Nov. 14, 1849.

Herbert Eugene Watkins, born Dec. 16, 1850.

CHILDREN OF MARY ANN BRIDGES.

MARY ANN BRIDGES, born May 4, 1832. Lives in Norwich, Ct. Married John H. Hough, Mar. 13, 1851.

George Appleton Hough, born Jan. 21, 1852, died Apr. 10, '54.
Dwight Hinkley " born Sep. 6, 1854.

FIFTH GENERATION.

CHILD OF SIMEON CUTLER.

SIMEON CUTLER, born July 12, 1811. Lives in Holliston. Married Mary Jane Nourse, Nov. 7, 1839.

Sarah Jane Cutler, born July 31, 1842.

CHILDREN OF ABNER H. CUTLER.

ABNER H. CUTLER, born May 7, 1815. Lives in Holliston. Married Persis Wardsworth, May 9, 1839.

Sophia Cutler, born Feb. 21, 1840—died Jan. 3, 1842.
Lorenzo " born June 14, 1845.
Albion Martin " born Dec. 11, 1849.

CHILD OF JOSEPHUS W. CUTLER.

JOSEPHUS W. CUTLER, born Feb. 19, 1817. Lives in Holliston. Married Phila E. Pierce, June 16, 1842.

Mary Helen Cutler, born Nov. 28, 1844.

CHILD OF MARTIN L CUTLER.

MARTIN L. CUTLER, born Oct. 16, 1819. Lives in Albany, New York. Married Maria A. Salisbury, May 20, 1851.

Walter S. Cutler, born Oct. 14, 1853.

CHILD OF TIMOTHY ROCKWOOD CUTLER.

TIMOTHY ROCKWOOD CUTLER, born May 3, 1822. Lives in Albany, New York. Married Rebecca Hillman, July 21, 1850.

Ida Sophia Cutler,	born Oct. 6, 1851.

Rebecca H., wife of Timothy R. Cutler, died suddenly, Dec. 21, 1853.

FOURTH GENERATION.

CHILDREN OF EZRA ROCKWOOD.

EZRA ROCKWOOD, born Nov. 5, 1784. Lived in Hopkinton. Married Polly Stone, 1808. Died suddenly, May 1, 1850.

Joann Rockwood,		born 1809.
Appleton	"	born 1811—died 1812.
Amos	"	born 1813—died 1814.
Sewall	"	born 1815—died 1815.
Ezra B.	"	born 1816.

Polly S., wife of Ezra Rockwood, died 1817.

Ezra Rockwood, married Betsey Stone, 1818.

Nathan Perry Rockwood,	born 1819.

The following sketch of the life of Ezra Rockwood, was kindly furnished by Rev. J. C. Webster, of Hopkinton.

Private worth alone attracts but little attention from the mass of the world. It is seldom recognized unless associated with learning, riches or heroism. Humble piety, for the most part, is unseen and unknown beyond a limited sphere. Its influence, like the fragrance of flowers in some sequestered dell, seems to spend itself on the desert air. Yet, like that very fragrance wafted by the breeze over the hills and plains, it is often carried by the Spirit of God to distant regions. And although its origin is unknown and unhonored by men, its effect is to counteract the moral contagions and alleviate the sorrows of mankind. While, therefore, our vanity may crave the show of riches, and our ambition the celebrity of rank for a departed friend, our pure Christian affection is satisfied with his genuine moral goodness. It is enough to be able to say of him, with truth and confidence, that he was a *good man.*

Such a man was Mr. Ezra Rockwood. He pursued, with much credit to himself, the high and honorable calling of a New England farmer. And his house and premises were always a pattern of neatness and order, that rendered them a delightful resort for his friends. He possessed a naturally mild and amiable disposition. Consequently he lived at peace with his neighbors, and was universally respected as a citizen by his townsmen. He was a kind and faithful husband; a judicious and affectionate father: and before he made any public profession of religion he was puritanic in the government of his family. He required of its members a strict observance of the annual Fast and Thanksgiving, as well as the weekly Sabbath. If they could go to town meetings and attend to their usual business, he would take no excuse for their absence from the sanctuary: and if the rain was likely to injure their best apparel, they must put on an inferior suit.

He was a good parishioner. He was the fast friend of his minister, to whom he frequently manifested his attachment by substantial tokens of friendship. Few did more in this way to win a pastor's love and attention. He was also invariably the firm supporter of the common interests of the parish. He, from principle, always shared its responsibilities as an active member. He never "signed off" to get rid of his taxes, or because his notions or personal wishes could not always be gratified.

But the crowning excellence of his character consisted in his unobtrusive and consistent piety. He united with the the Congregational Church in Hopkinton in 1832, at the age of 48. He never put himself forward, neither did he lag behind. He sought no office, but was content with the portion that providence assigned him. He was habitually honest in his dealings and business matters. Seldom, if ever, was there a charge of immorality brought against him. Integrity, with him, was an essential and practical Christian virtue. He never calumniated, yet he was quick to see and mourn over moral delinquencies wherever exhibited.

He loved the worship of his Maker. Though he lived two miles from the sanctuary, his seat was seldom vacant. He was an attentive listener to the word. He was generally also in his place at the conference meeting. His own house, too, was always open for the meeting for social prayer: and whether delegate or not, it was his custom, unless providentially hindered, to attend the semiannual meetings of the "Conference of Churches," and other public religious bodies in his neighborhood. Thus he kept himself informed of the Christian enterprises of his times.

In short, Mr. Rockwood's religious sentiments, sympathies and general conduct were right and Christian. He was on the right side in questions that involved the great interests of morality, humanity and the Church of Christ. While he manifested no lack of independence, he was pliable and reasonable. Indeed, there are few to whom we may, with more propriety, apply the words of the apostle, "pure, peaceable, gentle, easy to be entreated, full of mercy and good fruits, without partiality and without hypocrisy."

FIFTH GENERATION.

CHILDRN OF JOANN ROCKWOOD.

JOANN ROCKWOOD, born 1809. Lives in Hopkinton. Married Aaron Adams, 1828.

Amos Rockwood Adams, born 1830.		
Mary E.	"	born 1833.
Sabrina	"	born Oct. 6, 1834.
Eda	"	" Sep. 8, 1840—died Oct. 1, 1840.
Henry	"	born Oct. 18, 1841.

SIXTH GENERATION.

CHILD OF MARY E. ADAMS.

MARY E. ADAMS, born 1833. Lives in Jay, Me. Married Solomon N. Keyes, May 12, 1852.

Joana Rockwood Keyes, born March 10, 1853.

FIFTH GENERATION.

CHILDREN OF EZRA B. ROCKWOOD.

EZRA B. ROCKWOOD, born in 1816. Lives in Ashland. Married Esther M. Davenport, May 16, 1839.

Polly Stone Rockwood,	born Dec. 11, 1840.
Sarah Elizabeth "	born March 4, 1843.
Maria Louisa "	born Aug. 12, 1845.
Abbie Olivia "	born Sep. 9, 1847.
Emily F. "	born Oct. 14, 1851.

CHILDREN OF NATHAN P. ROCKWOOD.

NATHAN P. ROCKWOOD, born 1819. Lives in New York City. Married Mary A. Eames, April 8, 1845.

Cyrus Perry Rockwood, born Aug. 22, 1847.
Mary Eloise, " born July 19, 1849—died Dec. 4, 1851

FOURTH GENERATION.

CHILDREN OF MILLY ROCKWOOD.

MILLY ROCKWOOD, born Dec. 26, 1786. Married Elihu Whiting, April 7, 1808. Died Aug. 1, 1839. Lived in Barre.

Emeline Whiting,	born Sept., 1810.
Wm. Rockwood "	born Dec. 1814.

Elihu Whiting, died Nov. 11, 1838, aged 54.

FIFTH GENERATION.

CHILDREN OF EMELINE WHITING.

EMELINE WHITING, born Sept., 1810. Married Hiram Harwood, April 2, 1832. Lives in Barre.

Leander Harwood,	born Aug. 10, 1834.
Amos Whiting Harwood,	born June 4, 1838.
Hiram Sibley "	born July 27, 1845.

CHILDREN OF WILLIAM WHITING.

WILLIAM WHITING, born Dec., 1814. Married Betsey Green, April 2, 1835. Lives in Barre.

Harriet Augusta Whiting,	born May 18, 1836.
Olive Jane "	born May 27, 1840.
Albert Elmon "	born Aug. 15, 1846.

FOURTH GENERATION.

CHILDREN OF TIMOTHY ROCKWOOD.

TIMOTHY ROCKWOOD, born Jan. 17, 1789. Lived in Holliston. Married Polly Chamberlain, May 9, 1811. Died June 17, 1855.

Angeline Rockwood,	born Sept 11, 1812.
Catherine "	born Nov. 22, 1813.
Josephus Wheaton "	" Sep. 9, 1816—died Oct. 13, 1842.

Polly C., wife of Timothy Rockwood, died July 18, 1821.

Timothy Rockwood, married Nancy Adams, 1822.

Benjamin Adams Rockwood, born Aug., 1823.
William Chamberlain, " born May 8, 1825, died Oct. 12, '26.

A short time previous to the death of Timothy Rockwood, he was asked if he had any communication to his relatives which he wished to convey to them through this book, (which was then in course of preparation.) "*Oh yes*," he replied with great effort, "*but you are too late.*" In great weakness, and in broken accents he then further said, "*my desire is, that they all may be made partakers of Christ's salvation.*" His earnest countenance betokened that he had more to say, but he was too near the spirit land. A large circle of relatives and friends followed his remains to the grave.

The following is the first of three verses, sung at his funeral before the sermon, from "Watts's Select Hymns." Hymn 453.

[TUNE — *Gethsemane.*]

"Lo! the prisoner is released,
Lightened of his fleshly load;
Where the weary are at rest,
He is gathered to his God."

The following sketch of the life and character of Timothy Rockwood, is an extract from the sermon preached at his funeral. It was kindly furnished by his pastor, J. T. Tucker, D.D., of Holliston.

DEACON TIMOTHY ROCKWOOD.

The life of our deceased fellow-citizen and brother, Dea. Timothy Rockwood, was passed and terminated in this town of his nativity. He was born in 1789. His parents, though not professedly Christians, were strictly Orthodox in their views of truth, which they inculcated in the family after the methods then prevalent throughout this region; adhereing, moreover, in the general training of their children to the severe, yet wholesome simplicity of the former New England culture. Thus, at twenty years of age, our friend was sharply reproved by his father for going out on Sunday to take a pleasure-walk. This will show us where we have drifted from with respect to both the *fourth* and *fifth* commandments. Without endorsing by this remark all the opinions of that age, I wish to say, in passing, that we have fallen into a very lax habit as to the restraining of the young from Sabbath-recreations, and that we have subsided yet more from the true idea of filial subjection to parental authority. Our young men and maidens contrive to slip the yoke considerably sooner, in too many cases, than the second decade. The consequences are manifestly and manifoldly ruinous. This must not be held as indicating any lack of spirit in the youth of that day. Our friend's opening manhood was marked by rather an unusual development of personal activity. His temperament was lively, energetic, tending decidedly to a leading influence in matters of social interest, as for example, in military affairs to which he was considerably devoted, and in which he obtained a somewhat early promotion. I mention this, because it stands in quite peculiar connection with his conversion to Christ. The circumstances of this change in his life were these: He was 32 years old. It was the night after a large military parade. He had returned home fatigued with the excitements of the day and had retired to rest. After awhile a voice awoke him, which he was greatly surprised to find was that of his wife now dead, praying earnestly by his bedside for his salvation. She had been brought under conviction of sin, and had, about a fortnight before, found peace in believing; but this was his first knowledge of her religious solicitude. That was a solemn voice, in the hushed darkness — the wife of his youth interceding for her husband's soul at the end of this day of noise and temptation. Perhaps her heart told her that there was more than common need to pray for him whose pathway was entering perilously the enemy's land. That night was the turning-point of his career.

This unexpected discovery of his wife's conversion aroused him to a deep personal anxiety for his own salvation. But he made no disclosure of his concern of mind. For two weeks he was in great trouble of heart, wandering away from his employment into the woods several times a day for prayer, suffering severely under a consciousness of guilt and ruin, struggling now against God, and now after him. An old tree, beside which these petitions were mostly offered, he long remembered and cherished as the only earthly witness of his griefs and fears. But the light dawned in a few weeks, and it dawned clearly. This was in the year 1821, under the pastorate of the Rev. Josephus Wheaton.

Times were very different then from now. There were but eleven male members in this church. Conversions were infrequent. These, of two active, influential, middle-aged persons, produced no small sensation in this then quiet village, and several additional cases of the same kind followed quite closely. Mr. Rockwood and his wife in a few months made a public profession of their faith in Christ. The heart of their beloved pastor was encouraged, and his hands were strengthened. The Monday morning after that event, our brother commenced household devotions — an act which required some decision, as he had a large family of workmen and apprentices, who, however, habitually and cheerfully attended these exercises. I may here mention, that though his father did not belong to the church, he had maintained this domestic practice also. Thus doubtlessly making the duty still more obvious to the now-professing son. How beautiful this fireside worship of God, hallowing the sacred pleasure of home from generation to generation!

Our brother was elected to the office of deacon in this church, Sept. 27, 1830. His character as a Christian was of a strong and reliable cast; a little stern, it may be, compared with the present prevailing type, yet none the worse, perhaps, for that. The vigorous promptness of his natural manhood infused his piety with a resembling energy, and made him decided in counsel and firm in action. He was not a man of half views or measures where the church was concerned. It was with him habitually a paramount object of consideration. He greatly valued its institutions, its ordinances, discipline, and means of grace. He felt a kind of ecclesiastical responsibility and sense of honor — a soldier-like charge, I may say, with reference to the defence and welfare of the church, which is not so common as is desirable, among even those who bear its official trusts. Hence he was a good helper in the Lord, a substantial arm to lean upon, a laborer steadily at his post and well prepared for effective service.

Not a little of this effectiveness came from our brother's well-considered acquaintance with religious truth and duty. He was a very Scriptural Christian. He had studied the Bible with care and success as revealing both doctrinally and practically the will of God. He knew what was in it, and where it was to be found. Nothing was pleasanter to him than to teach a Bible-class; and this he did quite up to his last sickness. He was qualified to give instruction out of the Sacred Word, for it had been his teacher. It had taught him his theology more than had any human system of philosophy. He was well versed, also, in the principles and practice of church-government and order; and had a reason to give for the external faith which he loved and administered, as well as for the inward trust which he reposed in God.

Dea. Rockwood was esteemed and honored as a citizen. Very many lads were trained by him to mechanical industry, who have lived to be thankful for the strict vigilance with which he fulfilled these duties. Not always prosperous in all his business pursuits, he passed the ordeal of ill-fortune as uninjured as is perhaps to be expected in a world like this. He was a sympathising and helpful neighbor; a public-spirited and ready co-operator in social progress. Afflicted with ill-health through a large part of his days, bringing on a premature old age, he nevertheless has been one of our most busy and useful men, accomplishing an amount of labor surpassed by but a few.

For a year past a slow, consuming disease has been taking down his mortal tabernacle. This final sickness was with our brother a season of thoughtful, solemn setting his house in order for the summons of death. Relieved of all worldly anxieties through a kind providence for which he often expressed a deep thankfulness, he had little to do but to prepare for the expected change and then to wait for it with patient hope. In those quiet months, suffering from no distressful pains, and with a reason unclouded to the last, he deliberately went over the experience of his Christian life; sounded again the foundation on which it was built; took up the great elemental doctrines of his faith and love, and re-studied them prayerfully in the awful presence of eternity. The result was satisfactory. The whole structure of his piety gained strength and confidence from this review. His soul enjoyed a steadfast, tranquil rest in the promises of God. Conscious of many sins and deep unworthiness, he was enabled to realize the joy of forgiveness and acceptance through the Redeemer. His remnant on earth was blessed to the end with this unruffled peace in God. At length too feeble for any other religious exercise, he was reduced to a silent communion with heaven in mental devotion and the memory of familiar passoges of the Bible. His patience did not fail him; yet the last few weeks were a longing to depart from the wearisomeness of extreme debility, and to be with Christ. He died in unfailing hope, on Monday, the 18th inst., at the age of sixty-six.

You who here mourn his loss, the widowed companion of his last thirty years, his children, grand-children, and those who are bereaved of a dear brother and valued friend — you need no further proof than his living and his dying days to assure you that "precious in the sight of the Lord" has been his death. He has finished his work; he has entered into rest. The consolations of God which sustained his soul are left to support and comfort you to-day around his grave. Draw largely upon them. Your venerated relative is gone; but Christ and the promises endure; the covenant, on which his trust was planted, can also secure you in God's eternal love. Your dust will soon sleep beside his in yonder place of sepulchres, — room near there awaits you, where a long line of your ancestry has returned to clay. So through the faith which saved him may your spirits find room and habitation near his mansion, in heaven, when a few more suns have set, if you will but follow him as he followed Christ.

Another pillar, too, of our earthly temple of the Lord is removed to stand henceforth in "the house not made with hands." That familiar form, so long accustomed to wait on the church below, with the sacred vessels of the sanctuary will no more minister along these aisles, will no more give us aid and counsel in watching the Lord's flock in these pastures of his grace. He has gone to meet the pastors, and deacons, and members of this church, who have gone before, to report, perhaps, how God is loved and served in this his ancient dwelling-place; to sit at their table and Christ's in the New Jerusalem; to make another sainted worshipper before the throne of the Lamb. Richly are we represented there. How is Christ and heaven represented here? Would that we knew it as we should, that this communion of Christians is the repository of God's choicest grace, to be disbursed through prayer and holy faithfulness to all the living dying ones around us. Here does he gather the costliest treasures of his mercy to be distributed to all the needy by his people's consecrated hands. And as another and another of these active hands and loving hearts are palsied, stilled in death, He calls us, who should never call in vain, to do with the more diligence what remains for us to do, ere our sun set also in the night which shall have no earthly morning.

The following is the first of four verses of the funeral hymn, sung at the close of the sermon, from "Watts' Select Hymns." Hymn 231.

[TUNE — *Bristol.*]

"Unveil thy bosom faithful tomb,
Take this new treasure to thy trust,
And give these sacred relics room
To seek a slumber in the dust."

FIFTH GENERATION.

CHILDREN OF ANGELINE ROCKWOOD.

ANGELINE ROCKWOOD, born Sept 11, 1812. Lives in Holliston. Married Benjamin Hoffman, April 7, 1835.

Mary Maria Hoffman, born June 9, 1836.
George Storrs " " July 7, 1838--died Aug. 28, 1839.
George Rockwood " " Oct. 8, 1840.
Josephus Rockwood " " Nov. 7, 1845.

MARY M. HOFFMAN.

MARY M. HOFFMAN, married George Bartlett, Jan 10, 1855.

3

CHILD OF CATHERINE ROCKWOOD

CATHERINE ROCKWOOD, born Nov. 22, 1813. Lived in Holliston. Married Seth C. Hawes, Oct. 24, 1833. Died Feb. 25, 1837.

William Rockwood Hawes,	born Feb. 10, 1837

CHILDREN OF BENJ. A. ROCKWOOD.

BENJ. A. ROCKWOOD, born Aug. 1823. Lives in Holliston. Married Adelia P. Payson, Nov. 25, 1847.

Helen Maria Rockwood,		born Aug. 29, 1849.
Josephine Eliza	"	born Dec. 8, 1850.
Anna Louisa	"	born June 25, 1852.
Adelia Frances	"	born March 26, 1854.

FOURTH GENERATION.

CHILDREN OF CALVIN ROCKWOOD.

CALVIN ROCKWOOD, born June 3, 1792. Lives in Holliston. Married Louisa How, April 9, 1813.

Charles	Rockwood,	born	June 28, 1814.
Margaret Parker	"	"	March 16, 1816.
Martin Brown	"	"	Nov. 24, 1817.
Jerusha Burnet	"	"	July 12, 1819.
Louisa	"	"	June 22, 1821.
Calvin	" jr.,	"	July 10, 1823.
Nancy How	"	"	Aug. 24, 1826—died Dec. 1847.
Mille Whiting	"	"	April 13, 1828—died Jan. 1, 1833.
Laura Matilda	"	"	May 20, 1830.
Edwin Francis	"	"	Dec. 2, 1835.

Calvin Rockwood is the youngest and only surviving child of Timothy Rockwood, born in 1751. Since Aug. 11, 1827, he has followed both his parents, six brothers, two sisters, and five beloved children to their last resting-place. Their ages ranged from five to eighty years.

" His eyes have seen the rosy light
  Of *youth's* soft cheek decay,
And fate descend in sudden night
  On *manhood's* middle day."

His eyes have seen three precious ones
  In *girlhood's* bliss and bloom,
Their bright, serene, unclouded suns
  Go down in death at noon.

His eyes have seen the *steps of age*
  Halt feebly to the tomb; —
'T is Christ can all his griefs assuage,
  And lead him to his home.

Mr. Rockwood has been regarded as a useful citizen in Holliston. He was first chosen to town office in 1823, and was selectman in 1833–8–9. For thirteen years he was in its service, closing with 1842. He represented the town in General Court in 1839. He has done an extensive business in boot and shoe manufacturing; but now lives a comparatively retired life.

Millie Whiting Rockwood, who died in 1833, was a promising child. But four days intervened from her school-days to her everlasting holiday.

FIFTH GENERATION.

CHILD OF CHARLES ROCKWOOD.

Charles Rockwood, born June 28, 1814. Lived in Holliston. Married Harriet Mellen, 1838. Died Feb. 16, 1842.

Adelia Maria Rockwood,	born May 17, 1838.

Charles Rockwood died of consumption. His last days were happy; and his last words were, "You must make a good girl of Adelia."

CHILDREN OF MARGARET P. ROCKWOOD.

Margaret P. Rockwood, born March 16, 1816. Married Mark Crosby, July, 1838. Died Oct. 29, 1848.

Albert Rockwood Crosby,		born June 19, 1839.
Mark	" jr.,	born Oct. 24, 1840.
Thomas	"	born July 31, 1844.
Margaret Jerusha Towne Crosby,		" Aug. 19, 1846.

Mrs. Crosby, after her marriage, resided in Eastham, Yarmouth, Chatham and Worcester. She died of consumption at the latter place. Agreeable to her request, the obsequies were performed at Holliston, the place of her nativity. She cheerfully left her children in the hands of God, while her weary spirit breathed itself away without a struggle, Oct. 29, 1848.

CHILDREN OF MARTIN B. ROCKWOOD.

MARTIN B. ROCKWOOD, born Nov. 24, 1817. Lives in Holliston. Married Joanna Hill, April 7, 1842.

Nancy Ella Rockwood,	born March 30, 1848.
Edgar Martin "	born July 4, 1854.

FOURTH GENERATION.

JERUSHA B. ROCKWOOD.

JERUSHA B. ROCKWOOD, born July 12, 1819. Lived in Holliston. Married Leonard Towne, Sept., 1843. Died Dec., 1845.

Mrs. Towne died of consumption. During her protracted sickness, she exhibited a Christian spirit, and we trust it was gain for her to die.

FIFTH GENERATION.

CHILD OF LOUISA ROCKWOOD.

LOUISA ROCKWOOD, born June 22, 1821. Lives in Boston. Married Mark Crosby, Sept., 1849.

Charles Rockwood Crosby,	born July. 10, 1850.

CHILDREN OF CALVIN ROCKWOOD, Jr.

Calvin Rockwood, Jr., born July 10, 1823. Lives in Windham, Ct. Married Helena Whiting, 1846.

Emma Eldora Rockwood,		born Sept., 1846.
Ellen Frances	"	born Sept., 1849.
Clara Louise	"	born Oct., 1853.

CHILD OF LAURA ROCKWOOD.

Laura Rockwood, born May 20, 1830. Lives in Holliston. Married Gardner Gaylord.

Marion Louise Gaylord, born March 30, 1855.

THIRD GENERATION.

CHILDREN OF ELIZABETH ROCKWOOD,

AND SECOND CHILD OF TIMOTHY ROCKWOOD, BORN IN 1727.

Elizabeth Rockwood, was born Dec. 23, 1753. Lived in Holliston. Died May 1, 1849.

She had 6 children, 34 grand-children, 57 great grand-children, and 7 great, great grand-children, of whom 2 children, 23 grand-children, 43 great grand-children, 6 great, great grand children are now living.

Elizabeth Rockwood, married Simeon Cutler, 1770.

1. Elihu Cutler, born May 25, 1771.
2. Martin " " Dec. 28, 1773.
3. Uriel " " Feb. 27, 1776.
4. Ursula " " Aug 29, 1779.
5. Sally " " March 4, 1782 — died May 2, 1804.
6. James " " Dec. 9, 1785.

Mrs. Elizabeth Rockwood was the third daughter of Timothy Rockwood, born 1727, and the oldest of his lineage. She received a common school, and a good domestic education. At the age of seventeen years, there devolved on her the entire management of housekeeping and household affairs. She settled but half a mile from the place of her birth, where *her home was unchanged for seventy-nine years*, although a new house was built in the place of her first residence. After her decease, it passed into the possession of her descendants; and it remained so for a time, but is now owned and occupied by "outsiders." Relative to it, every thing is changed, though the majestic elms stand yet as pensive mourners — their shadows typical of the ever-changing scenes which have transpired within their precincts.

Mrs. Cutler was invariably *an early riser*, thus imitating the good habit of her early ancestry. She possessed a remarkably active and ardent temperament, and although it is always impossible to be in more than one place at a time, yet *she* would often more than half *seem* to be. She always had at hand a supply of general knowledge, and was apt to communicate — so much so, that, towards the close of life, her loquacity was oftentimes wearisome. The scenes of the Revolutionary War she would vividly portray to you. She loved to tell of her pastime, spent in horseback-rides and spinning-bees, — relative to the former, herself and friend would be seated together on the same pillion; the collation of the latter consisting of homely bean-porridge and brown bread. She often contrasted her youthful days with the present ones, and was frequently troubled on account of their apparent degeneracy.

Our relative unquestionably accomplished a great amount of good — "her life being a continual series of useful and benevolent acts." With her neighbors and relatives she was a "Florence Nightingale," willing to sacrifice almost anything to alleviate the sick and afflicted.

She died May 1st, 1849, aged 96 years, four months and eight days. She lived 13 years eight months and twenty-four days of holy time. The allegorical portrature of old age, so beautifully depicted in the twelfth chapter of Ecclesiastes, was exemplified during the last years of her life; happy that her dust could return to the earth as it was, and her spirit unto God who gave it.

Col. Simeon Cutler, her husband, died July 13, 1798, aged 49.

FOURTH GENERATION.

CHILDREN OF ELIHU CUTLER.

Elihu Cutler, born May 25, 1771. Lives in Holliston. Married Levina Newton, Nov. 25, 1798.

Simeon Newton Cutler,		born	Sept. 28, 1799.
Betsey Rockwood	"	"	Aug. 22, 1801.
Sally Newton	"	"	Nov. 13, 1803.
Elihu	" jr.,	"	Dec. 6, 1806.
Charles A.	"	"	Sept. 26, 1814.

Levina N. wife, of Elihu Cutler, died March 19, 1833.
Elihu Cutler, married Persis Phipps, Dec. 4, 1844.

Hon. Elihu Cutler, Esq., is the oldest living descendant of our worthy progenitor. In the year 1771, methinks we see him a bright-eyed little boy—an only son, the father's pride, and the mother's joy. Verily we can say of him now, he has seen a long life, chequered around with light and shade. As in his youth, so now, the stately elms rustle beside his door; their luxuriant foliage, as year by year renewed, is a fit emblem of the unnumbered blessings which have ever strewed his pathway. That he has also experienced many of the sor rows and trials of life, the death of many of his children and grand children in the morning and prime of life and usefulness, plainly and painfully show.

Though naturally of a slender constitution, he, in the aggregate, has enjoyed tolerably good health; and his longevity may, with great truthfulness, be attributed to his *strict adhereance to the laws of physiology*. He was blessed, and has uniformly cultivated a remarkably *calm* and *even temperament*. He is decidedly *regular* and *systematic* in all he does. The young may learn from his example how to cultivate the choice blessings of a calm and quiet old age. Ever since early manhood, he has evinced a great interest for the public good, and has long enjoyed the confidence and esteem of a large community extending far beyond the boundaries of his native town. He has been the administrator of forty-five estates; was a member of the Massachusetts Convention in 1820, to revise the Constitution; a representative in the General Court in 1827–8, and for four successive years, commencing with the year 1831, was senator for the county of Middlesex.

Our relative has long served the public with great fidelity. He has filled more offices of honor and trust, conferred on him by the town and by private individuals, than most men of his day. He is now passing down the steep declivity of life. May his relatives imitate his virtues.

Betsey R. Cutler, the surviving daughter of Hon. Elihu Cutler, Esq., has been an invalid nearly thirty-five years. But few have experienced more bodily suffering; and it has ever been united with composed resignation. She has, in a peculiar manner, received the care and sympathy of her father; and now, in his old age, it is becoming more and more reciprocal. She has also shared largely the esteem and kind regard of her brothers and sisters. Her advice and judgment is often sought for and heeded in the family.

FIFTH GENERATION.

CHILDREN OF SIMEON N. CUTLER.

Simeon N. Cutler, born Sept. 28, 1799. Lives in Ashland. Married Mary Fitts, Nov. 8, 1821.

Ellen Maria Cutler,	born	Nov. 30, 1822.
George Edmand "	"	Aug. 22, 1824.
William Henry "	"	July 21, 1826.
Delia Levina "	"	May 2, 1829.
Martha Jerusha "	"	Aug. 1, 1832.
Cornelius Howard "	"	Sept. 18, 1834.
William Clark "	"	May 17, 1837.
Charles F. "	"	July 22, 1841.

Simeon N. Cutler was a resident of Holliston till about the year 1837. He has been, for one or more sessions, a representative from Ashland in the Legislature. "He possesses in a large degree the characteristics of his aged father."

SIXTH GENERATION.

CHILD OF ELLEN M. CUTLER.

Ellen M. Cutler, born Nov. 30, 1822. Lived in Ashland. Married Joseph Ballord, Nov. 30, 1842. Died Aug. 6, 1845.

Mary Elizabeth Ballord, born July 5, 1844—died Aug. 26, '45.

CHILDREN OF GEORGE E. CUTLER.

George E. Cutler, born Aug. 22, 1824. Lives in Ashland. Married Cornelia E. Eames, Nov. 4, 1847.

Ellen Maria Cutler, born Apr. 20, 1851.
Eva Ophelia " " Feb. 27, 1853.

CHILD OF WILLIAM H. CUTLER.

William H. Cutler, born July 21, 1826. Lives in Ashland. Married Harriet R. Dennis, Sept. 7, 1851.

Maria Louisa Cutler, born August 7, 1852.

CHILD OF DELIA L. CUTLER.

Delia L. Cutler, born May 2, 1829. Lived in Ashland. Married Joshua Smith, Aug. 1, 1850. Died June 26, 1853.

Mary Lourina Smith, born Oct. 20, 1851.

STANZAS,

On the death of Mrs. Delia Levina Smith, wife of Mr. Joshua Smith, and daughter of Mr. S. N. Cutler, who died in Ashland June 26, 1853.

" Parent, by thy counsels moulded
Her's hath been the better part,
Many a gentle word lies folded
Warmly treasured in thy heart,
She hath left thy soul in shadows;
She hath wandered out of sight;
But she will return at night,
Bringing from celestial meadows,
Many a flower — a thought of light!

Sister, wherefore art thou weeping ? —
Joyously, at fall of day,
In pilgrim garb she took her way,
While glory, as from Heaven sent,
Shone all around her as she went!
Angel bands their watch are keeping;
Sister, wherefore art thou weeping ?

Husband, o'er thee hangs a cloud,
Shadow on thy hearth is lying;
By thee stands a vacant chair,
And alone thou sittest there
To hear her gentle accents, trying
Or her footsteps on the stair!
She is not dead, but gone before,
And stands on Jordan's farther border,
There, she waits thy coming o'er,
There, she will meet thee at the door
With her heavenly house in order!

Daughter, yet too young to know
The loss that has befallen thee!
While other hearts are beating low,
Thine with joy doth overflow,
And all thy tones, are tones of glee;

Thine, be the shining path she trod,
Thine, her faith, her hope, her God;
And unto thee the boon be given,
Who lost on earth a mother's care,
To meet her where the angels are,
And know a mother's love in heaven."

FIFTH GENERATION.

CHILDREN OF SALLY N. CUTLER.

SALLY N. CUTLER, born Nov. 13, 1803. Lived in Medway. Married James B. Wilson, Dec. 3, 1824. Died May 1, 1849.

Jane Lavinia Wilson, born March 10, 1827.
James Rufus " " Apr. 16, 1829—died Dec. 20, 1851.
Elihu Cutler " " June 26, 1831.
Charles Edward " " Oct. 15, 1835—died Aug. 25, 1836.
Helen Maria " " July 1, 1838—died Sept. 30, 1838.
Isabella Black " " Aug. 29, 1841.
Jason Eugene " " Sept. 4, 1843.

The following is an extract from a sermon occasioned by the death of Mrs. Sally C. Wilson, delivered on the Sabbath following her death, by Rev. David Sanford, of Medway. The text was, "For me to live, is Christ; to die is gain."

"Ours is the duty and the privilege to gather Mrs. Wilson's excellencies as they were developed, so that we may cherish her spirit and, like her, find it gain to die. She was a *humble woman.* She saw and felt the plague of her own heart, and that view was abiding. It was a grace added to her native meekness. From the first emotion of trust in Christ, her confidence was uniform, unwavering and increasng. He was her 'wisdom, righteousness, sanctification andi redemption.' She longed to see the Son of God enthroned in all hearts and served by all mankind. *As a wife*, she was faithful, devoted, confiding. She was eminently useful in all matters the of household — was industrious, frugal, unwearied and persevering in her duties, and was prompt in all domestic arrangements. It was her motto, to have a place for everything, and everything in its place. *As a mother*, she was a pattern for other parents. She felt a deep interest in her children's temporal welfare; yet her great concern was, that that they might all choose that good part which cannot be taken from them. For this end she gave them up to God in baptism, and had the seal of his blessed covenant upon them. *As a member of the Church of Christ*, he was consistent, faithful, watchful and useful. Her views were enlarged and her affections expanded. While she loved all, those most devout and prayerful were her choicest friends. She had kindness of feeling and action towards all; was ever ready to relieve the wants of the destitute and to do all in her power to minister to their comfort. She took the most favorable view of the character of others — slow to condemn, and prepared to make allowance for circumstances, and to reclaim those who were out of the way. The language of divine truth was verified in her — 'When a man's ways please the Lord, he maketh even his enemies to be at peace with him.'

Such being her exit and such her traits of character, we are assured it was gain for her to die. We are henceforth to view her among the *living ones* in the 'spirit world,' forever freed from sin in the full fruition of the blessed presence and glorious image of her Divine Redeemer.

May her mantle fall emphatically upon surviving relatives. May we all cherish her spirit, and like her, live to Christ."

FIFTH GENERATION.

JANE L. WILSON.

JANE L. WILSON, born March 10, 1827. Lives in Brooklyn, N. Y. Married Gilbert E. Daniels, Nov. 28, 1853.

CHILDREN OF ELIHU CUTLER, Jr.

ELIHU CUTLER, JR., born Dec. 6, 1806. Lived in Holliston. Married Rebeckah Temple, April 25, 1830. Died April 19, 1855.

Elbridge Jefferson	Cutler,	born 1831.
Jason Temple	"	born Feb. 17, 1834—died Apr. 21, '43.
Arthur Eugene	"	" Oct. 24, 1837—died Sept. 1, 1842.
Elihu 2d	"	" Nov. 3, 1841—died Nov. 6, 1842.
Helen Francis	"	" June 26, 1844—died Jan. 23, 1845.
Arthur Hamilton	"	" Jan. 26, 1849.

The following sketch of the life and character of Hon. Elihu Cutler, jr., is abridged from an Obituary, published soon after his death, in the *Milford Journal:*

"Hon. Elihu Cutler, jr., the second son of Hon. Elihu Cutler, was born in Holliston, Dec. 6, 1806, and died April 19, 1855. He received a good common school and academical education, and early engaged in the business of manufacturing; in the different branches of which he was extensively and successfully employed up to the close of his life. Nature endowed him with a mind of much more than ordinary powers and susceptibilities, which faithful and judicious training prepared him for an extent of usefulness and influence among his fellowmen, seldom attained in the common walks of life. He uniformly exhibited a lively interest in the cause of education, in the maintenance of good morals, and in all real objects of philanthropy. Every enterprise tending to the prosperity and happiness of our people, received his willing and generous co-operation and support. His personal and political friends would always confide safely in his integrity and the wisdom of his counsels. The people appreciated his worth, and bestowed on him, unsought for, almost every office in their gift, and confided to him their most important trusts, and in no instance was their confidence misplaced. In the autumn of 1853, he was elected to the Senate of the Massachusetts Legislature for 1854 — the duties of which office he discharged with signal ability and success."

Elbridge J. Cutler, the son of Hon. Elihu Cutler, jr., graduated at Harvard in 1849 with high honors. He is proficient in whatever he undertakes — is a young gentleman of superior literary acquirements. Moreover, is a poet; and his attainments herein are already considerably known. He has delivered several poems at public gatherings — the last at Cambridge, at last Commencement. The following are some extracts from it, published in the *Boston Daily Advertiser* of July 4:

"The President then introduced the Poet of the day, Elbridge Jefferson Cutler, Esq., of Holliston, from whose beautiful poem we have room only for the following brief extracts:—

Turn to the East,—what mystic splendors cling
Around the clime where all traditions spring,
Where Eden bloomed, where Eden's glories shine,
Where prophets walked, and bards of song divine;
Where in time's childhood, India's rarest gems
Clustered like stars in regal diadems,
And still the vine its cloistered arches weaves,
The purple grape looks out between the leaves,
And its dark cheek, like half repentant nun
Turns to the enamored kisses af the sun.

But wilder scenes arrest the mournful gaze,—
Vineyards laid waste, and hamlets in a blaze,
War spreads his terrors o'er that fair domain,
Shrieks in the air, or thunders on the plain.
Broad in the breeze the martial ensigns float,
Peals on the soldier's ear the bugle note,
Dim through the cloud, the burnished rifles shine,
As rank succeeds to rank, and line to line.

The greedy earth still pants for human gore,
Be men, to-day,—her lip shall ask no more,
Be men, and streams yet innocent of blood,
Shall moan at evening with a crimson flood.
So shall the laurels wet with such a dew
Of your immortal fathers, bloom anew!
Bid louder yet the clarion's note arise,
Thro' fire and smoke the meteor standard flies,
See! Glory plants her budding laurels there,
Smiles in the van, and waves her shining hair!

Oh! Night, meek-eyed and sad, a patient nurse,
On tip-toe goest thou about the earth

To soothe her grief, and close her bleeding wounds;
Upon thy bosom she weeps out her woe,
And whispers in thy ear, her tale of sin.

Gentle as some familiar melody
That steals into the current of our thoughts
Beguiling toil of pain and weariness,
Soft as the breathing of a sleeping babe
Felt on the languid mother's wasted cheek,
In the long watch of pain beside the couch,
When life lights up again the glassy eyes,
And all her being warms with speechless love;
So soft, so gentle, comes the evening wind,
Like words of pardon whispered out of Heaven,
To kiss away the sulphurous cloud of war.
The moon is risen, and the numerous waves
Catch her cool light in crystal chalices,
And murmur welcome all along the shore.
But here her beams fall on the broken sword,
The aimless rifle and the bayonet,
And the dead soldier's wide, lack-lustre eye.
The bed of glory is a bed of pain.
The air is filled with shuddering groans, and cries
Of agony wrung from the coward lips
In mockery of the brave heart within.

Nor these alone. For woman's voice is there,
And woman's footsteps light upon the grass
In angel ministration. And white hands
Bind up the soldier's wounds, and pour the balm,
And offer cordials to the livid lips,
Cool the pained brow, and chafe the feverish palm.

Perhaps the touch transports his heart away
To Seine, or Rhone, or Shannon, or the Tweed,
And in his cottage home, he seems to lie.
He feels a wife's warm hand upon his brow,
He hears the cadence of a mother's voice,
And the young children prattle at the door.

Amid it all, in coral undertone
The river's dashings creep upon his ear
And the old sunlight golden's on the wall.
Then with the scene, the fight is strangely mixed;
And with a shout half triumph and half wail,
And with a smile, as when a sunsets's beam
Shines white upon December's snowy hills,
'We have fought gloriously! I must rest.'
So in that blissful dream, the soldier dies.

Go ask the ages for a deed like this,
Call from her crumbled tomb, Semiramis,
Place in the list, wild Parthia's warlike queen,
The Spartan mother, and the Palmyrene,
With all bright names, — their proudest honors pale
Beside the simple wreath of Nightingale!
No glittering train attends her on her way,
No screaming horn, no banner streaming gay,
She bears no sword, yet binds around her hair,
Plucked in that laureled field, the brightest laurel there.

Oh! woman, what varieties are these, —
Soother of pain and ornament of ease,
A reed in weakness, in that weakness strong,
The soldier's watchword and the theme of song,
A blessed star to man in kindness given,
Whose light illumines earth, whose home is heaven!

The following were the concluding lines of the poem:

To-day is man's; the Past and Future, God's.
All the hoar ages died to give it birth,
And all the Future hangs upon its deed.
Morn, launching from the green horizon's shore
His radiant bark, while all the forest tips
And all the air are bright with pennons gay,
Calls to his twilight sister round the world,
'To-day! To-day!' And she with rosy cheek

Waves white-armed farewell from her dusky car,
While like a setting star, behind the hills,
Her voice sinks silverly, 'To-day, to-day!'
Earth takes the warning on her thousand tongues.
The little flowers whose duty is to bloom,
The busy streams that bear away the hills,
Ocean with all his harmony of shells,
And mountain torrents, shout aloud, 'To-day!'

This is the strain to which the forests bowed,
And gray old mountains bounded like the roe.
This is the charm that turned Amphion's reed,
Gave life to stones, and raised the Theban walls.
This is the magic of Aladdin's ring:
The noble music of all worthy deeds!

Hear it, oh heart! Throw doors and windows wide,
And let the light and voice of morning in!
Who careth where the shades of night are fled?
Who waits To-morrow's far uncertain dawn!
To-day, to-day, the sun is on the hills.
Go forth, oh, hero! resolute and strong.
Work while the day is given, and working, sing.
And though amid the clashing instruments
Of earth's great orchestra, men heed it not,
No feeblest voice shall pass unheard of God!"

FIFTH GENERATION.

CHILD OF CHARLES CUTLER.

Charles Cutler, born Sept. 25, 1814. Lived in Grafton. Married Mary A. G. Strickland, March 5, 1837. Died Dec. 20, 1839.

Caroline Elizabeth Cutler, born Sep. 1839—died Dec. 31, '42.

The following extracts are from Obituaries published soon after his decease, in the *Boston Recorder* and *National Æegis*: —

"Died in Holliston, Dec. 20, at the residence of his father, Hon. Elihu Cutler, Esq., Charles Cutler, M. D., practicing physician in Grafton, New England Village, aged 25 years.

To an unusually amiable disposition by nature, we must add in our portrait of our deceased friend, more than an ordinary share of native talent; a naturally sound and well cultivated mind, active habits of mental labor, feelings naturally benevolent and quickly sympathetic.

Though 'young in years,' he was emphatically 'in experience ripe.' He had received his moral, as well as physical education, in the stern school of ill-health. From boyhood up, he had suffered from physical debility; and he seemed to live, as well as act, as if, (to use his own words to an intimate friend, a few weeks before his death,) 'his life was suspended by an unusually slender thread.' This fact, from a well known principle of human nature, might have endeared him to his friends; and perhaps the necessity of such care might have softened his manners: it increased their anxiety when he commenced his responsible profession.

The severity of physical treatment to which he had been compelled to subject himself, had served to give a philosophical turn of mind to one already so. His feelings, naturally ardent, had been thoroughly subjected to a severe regimen. His very thoughts were taught to flow in a proper channel; and it seemed to be as much a matter of *principle* to keep *them* within the boundaries of propriety as his actions. In the words of one who knew him well, 'he made the most of life,' as if he had the conviction always before him, that he should not live long; and he seemed by his perfect resignation to his lot to think, that

'That life is long which answers life's great end.'

His piety was thorough and habitual. It seemed to be a part of his being. He was pious from principle; and so unostentatious was he, that he seemed almost unconscious that he was the ardent Christian. There was no bigotry in his piety, and yet he was sternly pious; and seducing him from the practice of what he deemed his duty, would have been like seducing him from his favorite profession. He was the pious man everywhere. Gay as he often and generally was in conversation, this gaiety never degenerated unto rudeness; and *a breach of decorum was equivalent with him to a breach of duty.*

He was enthusiastic in his profession — very studious; and what is a legitimate inference from these premises, he was remarkably successful in practice, and his friends and acquaintances fondly predicted eminence in his profession. He had been but two years in New England Village, and yet his practice was so extensive that it required more of the physical man than he could summon to his aid.

His prospects for extended usefuleess were very animating, and they ever seemed to be clouded by the almost certainty that not far ahead was the termination of his earthly career. Amid the multitude of responsibilities imposed upon him by an extensive practice, he declared to one to whom he was accustomed to unbosom himself, that the cheering declaration, 'my grace is sufficient for thee,' was always enough to shed light in his path, and cheer and sustain him.

On his return to his parental home, at the annual festival of Thanksgiving, consumption, which had for years been preying upon him most strikingly, like 'a worm at the root,' and which by unusual care he had been able most manfully to resist, determined to finish its work. And this it was enabled to do in a few weeks in connection with a slight fever, contracted, perhaps, in his professional labor, and under which he suffered before his return to his friends. His death was the beautiful closing of such a life as he had lived — calm, serene, full of hope.

Towards the close of his life, his devotions were almost incessant; but finding at last by the beat of his pulse, which he deliberately compared with that of those around his bed, he bid adieu to his friends, and then turning to the partner of his joys and sorrows, he bid her an affectionate farewell with the simple exclamation, 'Mary, I am going; put your trust in God.' He fell asleep

> 'Like one who wraps the drapery of his couch about him
> And lies down to pleasant dreams.' "

FOURTH GENERATION.

CHILDREN OF MARTIN CUTLER.

MARTIN CUTLER, born Dec. 28, 1773. Lived in Holliston. Married Elizabeth Mellen, 1799. Died Jan. 7, 1845.

James Mellen Cutler,	born Aug., 1800.
Simeon "	" Aug. 20, 1802—died Dec. 28, 1802.
John Milton "	" Feb. 9, 1804.

Elizabeth M., wife of Martin Cutler, died Oct. 28, 1805.

Martin Cutler, married Sophia Holbrook, April, 1810.

Simeon Cutler,	born July 12, 1811.
Betsey Mellen Cutler,	" April 18, 1813.
Abner Holbrook "	" May 7, 1815.
Josephus Wheaton "	" Feb. 19, 1817.
Martin Luther "	" Oct. 16, 1819.
Timothy Rockwood "	" May 3, 1822.

Martin Cutler always lived upon the homestead of his father — an estate embracing many broad acres. He has seen many of the ups and downs of life ; was an active and laborious man. He was fond of having his hands full of business, and somewhat eccentric. Everybody called him uncle. He was a good neighbor.

Betsey M. Cutler was an invalid for many years. She has now, however, regained her health, and devotes much of her time in administering to the sick. In *business* engagements her word is reliable ; but relative to *pleasure*, she considers it only gabble. She became a member of the Congregational Church in 1832.

FIFTH GENERATION.

CHILDREN OF JAMES M. CUTLER.

James M. Cutler, born Aug., 1800. Lives in Holliston. Married Jemima Bullard, April 25, 1826.

Nelson James Cutler,	born July 9, 1827.
Henry Edmund "	" Sept. 26, 1831.
Albert Mellen "	" Oct. 23, 1833.
Ellen Jemima "	" Oct. 4, 1837.

NELSON JAMES CUTLER.

Nelson James Cutler, born July 9, 1827. Lives in Albany, N. Y. Married Sarah Fisher, July 9, 1855.

SIXTH GENERATION.

CHILD OF ALBERT M. CUTLER.

Albert M. Cutler, born Oct. 23, 1833. Lives in Boston. Married Emma S. Dodd, 1854.

Thomas Cutler born June 17, 1855.

FIFTH GENERATION.

CHILDREN OF JOHN M. CUTLER.

John M. Cutler, born Feb. 9, 1804. Lives in Holliston. Married Electa Burr, Oct. 21, 1830.

Eliza Ann	Cutler,	born	Aug. 19, 1831.
Caroline Frances	"	"	June 25, 1833—died Feb. 6, 1837.
Emma Burr	"	"	July 20, 1835.
George Milton	"	"	March 4, 1838—died Sept. 18, 1838.
Josephine	"	"	Sept. 7, 1839.
Geo. Washington	"	"	Jan. 7, 1842.
Caroline Mellen	"	"	Nov. 13, 1844.
Jane Louisa	"	"	Nov. 8, 1846.

SIXTH GENERATION.

CHILD OF ELIZA A. CUTLER.

Eliza A. Cutler, born Aug. 19, 1831. Lives in Holliston. Married Elbridge G. Whiting, Nov. 1, 1849.

Emma Louisa Whiting, born Sept. 18, 1852.

FIFTH GENERATION.

CHILD OF SIMEON CUTLER.

SIMEON CUTLER, born July 12, 1811. Lives in Holliston. Married Mary Jane Nourse, Nov. 7, 1839.

Sarah Jane Cutler, born July 31, 1842.

CHILDREN OF ABNER H. CUTLER.

ABNER H. CUTLER, born May 7, 1815. Lives in Holliston. Married Persis Wardsworth, May 9, 1839.

Sophia Cutler, born Feb. 21, 1840—died Jan. 3, 1842.
Lorenzo " " June 14, 1845.
Albion Martin " " Dec. 11, 1849.

CHITD OF JOSEPHUS W. CUTLER.

JOSEPHUS W. CUTLER, born Feb. 19, 1817. Lives in Holliston. Married Phila E. Pierce, June 16, 1842.

Mary Helen Cutler, born Nov. 28, 1844.

CHILD OF MARTIN L CUTLER.

MARTIN L. CUTLER, born Oct. 16, 1819. Lives in Albany, New York. Married Maria A. Salisbury, May 20, 1851.

Walter S. Cutler, born Oct. 14, 1853.

CHILD OF TIMOTHY ROCKWOOD CUTLER.

Timothy Rockwood Cutler, born May 3, 1822. Lives in Albany, New York. Married Rebecca Hillman, July 21, 1850.

Ida Sophia Cutler,	born Oct. 6, 1851.

Rebecca H., wife of Timothy R. Cutler, died suddenly, Dec. 21, 1853.

FOURTH GENERATION.

CHILDREN OF URIEL CUTLER.

Uriel Cutler, born Feb. 27, 1776. Lived in Holliston. Married Nabby Morse, April 25, 1809. Died Sept. 12, 1849.

An Infant,		born Feb. 22, 1810—died Feb. 24, 1810.
Ursula Cutler,		" Oct. 28, 1811.
Elizabeth Leland	"	" May 3, 1814.
Simeon Morse	"	" May 13, 1816.
In Infant Son		" June 22, 1818—died June 23, 1818.
Abigail	"	" Jan. 15, 1820.
Uriel, jr.	"	" May 13, 1822.
Alfred	"	" July 11, 1824.
Mary Lucretia	"	" May 25, 1829.

Mr. Uriel Cutler was a thriving farmer, and owned large property in real estate. He settled in Sherborn,

Mass., about the time of his marriage, where he lived thirty years, then returned to Holliston where he resided until his death. He left a good competence to his heirs, who are living in its peaceable enjoyment.

FIFTH GENERATION.

CHILDREN OF URSULA CUTLER.

URSULA CUTLER, born Oct. 28, 1811. Lives in Walpole, N. H. Married Orlando Leland, Jan. 1, 1839.

Isabella Cutler Leland,	born Nov. 24, 1840.
Lewis A. "	" Nov. 16, 1842.
Francis Orlando "	" Sept. 14, 1849.

CHILDREN OF ELIZABETH L. CUTLER.

ELIZABETH L. CUTLER, born May 3, 1814. Lives in Sherborn. Married Elijah P. Leland.

Elbridge Leland,	born, 1836.
Elizabeth "	" 1840.

CHILDREN OF SIMEON M. CUTLER.

SIMEON M. CUTLER, born May 13, 1816. Lives in Holliston. Married Elmira A. Bullard, Nov. 25, 1841.

Edward Morse Cutler,	born Nov. 30, 1844.
William Bullard "	" Dec. 13, 1846.
Mary Elmira "	" April 30, 1849.

Mr. S. Morse Cutler, snice 1841, has resided in Sherborn, Lockport, N. Y., and Holliston. He located at the latter place in 1844. He is an enterprising and thriving farmer, and is also distinguished for the attention he pays to the cultivation of fruit-trees and to horticulture.

FOURTH GENERATION.

ABIGAIL CUTLER.

Abigail Cutler, born Jan 15, 1820. Lives in Holliston. Married Otis B. Bullard, Jan. 11, 1843.

Mr. and Mrs. Bullard are excellent teachers of music — both vocal and instrumental. Holliston and many of its surrounding towns have been much instructed and benefitted by them in this science. During the past winter they have been teaching in Pennsylvania. Many, both adults and juveniles, will long cherish their memory and remember their instructions.

May the time never come when any of them shall hang their harps upon the willows!

FIFTH GENERATION.

CHILDREN OF URIEL CUTLER.

URIEL CUTLER, jr., born May 13, 1822. Lives in Holliston. Married Susan E. Lovering, May 29, 1849.

Newell Lovering Cutler, born Aug. 11, 1850.
Uriel Herbert " born Mar. 14, 1853—died Oct. 21, '54.
Uriel Waldo " born Nov. 1, 1854.

FOURTH GENERATION.

ALFRED CUTLER.

ALFRED CUTLER, born July 11, 1824. Lives in Holliston. Married Mary J. Mann, April 7, 1853.

FIFTH GENERATION.

CHILD OF MARY L. CUTLER.

MARY L. CUTLER, born May 25, 1829. Lives in Boston. Married Edmund F. Leland, Feb. 26, 1853.

Waldo Daniels Leland, born March 30, 1854.

FOURTH GENERATION.

CHILD OF URSULA CUTLER.

Ursula Cutler, born Aug. 29, 1779. Lived in Holliston. Married John Mellen, Nov. 28, 1799. Died Oct. 24, 1804.

James Mellen, born Apr. 30, 1804—died Oct. 1827.

FOURTH GENERATION.

CHILDREN OF JAMES CUTLER.

James Cutler, born Dec. 9, 1785. Lives in Holliston. Married Nancy Leland, 1813.

George Cutler,	born	March 30, 1814.
Francis	"	" Oct. 23, 1815.
Roswell	"	" July 26, 1817.
James	"	" Sept. 5, 1819.
Caroline	"	" June 15, 1821—died Sept. 17, 1833.
Adeline	"	" March 12, 1823—died Jan. 1, 1833.
J. Addison	"	" Feb. 15, 1825—died Sept. 12, 1853.
Willard	"	" Jan. 28, 1827.
A. Jackson	"	" Nov. 23, 1828—died Dec. 19, 1853.
Charles	"	" Nov. 6, 1835.

Mr. James Cutler is active, enthusiastic and affable. He has a remarkable talent for adapting himself to the wants and wishes of others. He has ever been a true

Hollistonian. In almost every movement for the public good, and to build up the town, he has been first and foremost — often making advances, which, for the time being seemed injurious to his own best interests. He built the "Winthrop House," and many other fine buildings were erected under his proprietorship. He is one who emphatically looks and longs for progress and improvement, both in men and things, and has lived to see many of his wisest and best predictions realized. May he yet live to see many more.

Mr. and Mrs. Cutler's family circle has been sorrowfully broken by the removal by death of two sons and two daughters. Both the sons died of consumption.

The following notices of the life and character of these four children, Caroline, Adeline, J. Addison and A. Jackson Cutler, were kindly furnished the compiler by the mother of these deceased: —

"When we recall to mind the incidents connected with the short, but interesting lives of those affectionate sisters, Caroline and Adeline Cutler, and contrast the scanty recourse available, (some twenty-five years ago,) with the more favored of the present time, we feel assured that *they* were indeed taught of the Spirit of God.

At the time of which we write, the young enjoyed few opportunities of hearing religious truth, except from the pulpit, and the teaching of the 'Assembly's Shorter Catechism,' which we think is better calculated to strengthen the memory, than to warm the heart, or instruct the minds of youth.

In the limited circle of their acquaintance, there seemed to be no one to lead their enquiring minds to Jesus, to portray his love to children, therefore, often they were found weeping in agony of spirit, feeling 'they were sinners.' They became praying children. When asked what they prayed for, replied, 'For a new heart.'

We cannot forbear mentioning their simple development of faith in God, in trivial circumstances of daily life — their recourse was to fall upon the knee for direction and support. On one occasion the youngest left the room, but soon returned with her countenance radiant with delight, saying, 'Mother, I felt cross, but have been praying, and now feel better.'

These affectionate hearts were moved at one time to agree together to offer daily prayer to God in their mother's behalf. But a short time before the youngest fell sick, she said to her sister, 'Have you forgot for one day our agreement? I can say I never have.'

Methinks we still hear the sweet melody of their voices, and feel assured that the words of a favorite hymn are ratified in heaven, —

'Then we shall see Jesus,
There be no more sinning,
When we shall all meet above.'

J. Addison Cutler was emphatically one of nature's noblemen — an *honest man* in every sense of the word. In infancy and in his youthful days, as in manhood, all esteemed his word as truth. Humble and retiring in his disposition, firm in purpose, energetic and persevering when enlisted, but cool and calculating in his deliberations, never starting until he fully understood his errand. Those who knew him best, considered him altogether an *original* character—ever anxious to hear, rather than to be heard. His words were few, and on no occasion were ever heard in slander, however others might differ from him in opinion; nor did he fear to rebuke it, when indulged in by those older than himself. Strangers thought him parsimonious. From the style of his dress, comfort and convenience were never neglected. He judged no man a gentleman from the richness of his attire. He desired more 'to be, than to seem to be.' Whenever he met with those whom he could by any means relieve or benefit, it gave him unalloyed pleasure, without desiring or expectiug reward, either in time or in eternity. His courage and activity retained him in business some years, when it might have been prudent to retire and seek relief from pain and suffering; but hope was strong within him, and he strove to reach the goal he had so long looked forward to as the haven of earthly rest.

Should any think this sketch an over-drawn portraiture, we might have copied from the effusions of other pens, for he had *many* friends that appreciated and loved him.

He gave up his business in the year 1853, and returned to his parental home, believing that spring and summer, with medical advice and active exercise in the open air, would invigorate, if not restore his general health.

He struggled long and manfully with the fell destroyer. Need we say it was hard to give up? Oh! how hard to give up what has been long looked forward to as the consummation of happineess, and feel that the one thing needful had been neglected. So he felt. He said to his pastor, not many weeks before death, 'I have always believed in a change of heart, and feel that I have never experienced that change.' From that time, he eagerly listened to religious instruction with his characteristic fixedness of purpose. In answer to the inquiry, 'if he prays to God for help,' he replied, 'yes, I have gone as far as my knowledge extends.' He received the counsel and prayers of his pious friends with gratitude to the last hour of his life. He said his mind was peaceful, and he desired his sick brother to be summoned to his bed-side, and exhorted him to seek religion.

A. Jackson Cutler possessed an elevated sense of moral responsibility, a lively imagination, united with an amiable disposition and a pleasing address, which gained him many warm and worthy friends. Vice he detested in every form; and it is believed he avoided every appearance of evil. His early impressions in keeping the Sabbath may be shown by it being required of him to travel once on that day. The excursion, it is believed, would, on any other day, have been received with enthusiastic delight; but the agony expressed on his saddened countenance, made an indelible impression on the writer's heart which time will never efface. He described his feelings on his return as fearful, looking for God's righteous judgments and an unsuccessful termination of his errand. This principle adhered to him through life; and he was never able to see how a Christian apothecary could make himself believe that a *duty*, which appeared to him merely a *pecuniary profit* He always expressed it his determination, when he could control a shop himself, that it should be accessible on the Sabbath, only to the sick and the suffering.

He enjoyed a healthy constitution, not to say robust, until a year's residence in Cincinnati, Ohio. There the climate, and the remedies prescribed for him, weakened his power of endurance; yet he appeared to regain his health, until a cold seated on his lungs, which he, in his inexperience did not consider of sufficient importance to leave unfulfilled a previous engagement, the more especially as his employer, in whose age and wisdom he confided, endeavored to dissipate all alarm and retain his services, until his inability compelled him to seek a refuge in his childhood's home, there to join his brother, to linger a few short months, and bid adieu to all his cherished hopes of success in a business life and the promised anticipation of domestic happiness.

He became convinced his days were numbered, and with a calm and clear intellect, turned his undivided attention to hearing the Word of God read; and the counsel and prayers of his pastor and a dear religious friend, were eagerly heard and acted upon. He was willing to give all up, and, said he, 'I know the Saviour *will* receive me,' not feeling that his merit, but a new heart, which God had given him had entitled him to an inheritance where all tears shall be wiped away."

FIFTH GENERATION.

CHILDREN OF GEORGE CUTLER.

GEORGE CUTLER, M. D., born March 30, 1814. Lives in Charlestown. Married Ann M. Smith.

Caroline Amelia Cutler,		born	Nov., 1847.
George	"	jr., "	July, 1852.
Maria Louisa	"	"	Oct., 1854.

George Cutler entered Brown University, in 1835, and received the diploma of A. B. in 1835. He is a practising physician in Charlestown, Mass.

FOURTH GENERATION.

FRANCIS CUTLER.

FRANCIS CUTLER, born Oct. 23, 1815. Lives in Holliston. Married Mary A. Patt, Sept., 1845.

Francis Cutler is a close imitator of the peculiar characteristics of his father. He has a calculating spirit and will make his mark in the world.

ROSWELL CUTLER.

ROSWELL CUTLER, born July 26, 1817. Lives in Boston. Married Caroline A. Fisk, Dec., 1853.

Docts. Roswell, and Willard Cutler, his brother, are Dentists. Office No. 25, Winter-St.

FIFTH GENERATION.

CHILD OF JAMES CUTLER.

JAMES CUTLER, jr., born Sept. 5, 1809. Lives in Boston. Married Louisa F. Morse, Nov. 4, 1846.

Abbott Wayland Cutler, born Oct. 10, 1850.

J. Cutler is proprietor of the Bonnet Bleachery, No. 22, Hanover-St. He is well worthy the patronge of all his female relatives, and that would be perfectly sufficient and satisfactory to him.

THIRD GENERATION.

CHILDREN OF DEBORAH ROCKWOOD,

AND FOURTH CHILD OF TIMOTHY ROCKWOOD, BORN IN 1727.

Deborah Rockwood, born Dec. 10, 1758. Lived in Holliston. Died Aug. 29, 1836.

She had 4 children, 9 grand-children, 31 great grand-children, and 4 great, great grand-children; of whom 8 grand-children, 26 great grand-children, and 4 great, great grand-children are now living.

Deborah Rockwood, married James Mellen, January, 1779.

1. Timothy Mellen, born April 29, 1780.
2. Elizabeth " " " " "
3. Deborah " " " 19, 1785—died Oct. 17, 1787.
4. James " " " 23, 1789—died Mar. 7, 1796.

A worthy, and venerable citizen, not of our lineage, has informed me that " Mrs. Deborah Mellen was very handsome, and her intellect above the mediocrity;" she was no school-teacher nor piano-forte player; but she it was who would make the air revirbirate with the merry sound of her spinning-wheel. Ever and anon were neatly arranged by her in the wide open cupboard, long rows of nicely polished pewter plates; the transparency of this ware being regarded in those days as an index of good house-keeping. Mrs. Mellen lived in the precarious time of the Revolution, and courageously and promptly administered to the necessities of those who fought for freedom. She made coats for the soldiers, and plied her needle for them with almost ceaseless industry. In many respects her life was camelion-like. A routine of duties devolved upon her, which but few have experienced. Her husband was for a time in the Revolutionary War, was subsequently chosen Captain, and at different periods of life sustained all the minor offices of the Militia. He was afflcted for thirty years with the shaking palsy, and for more than twenty years was utterly helpless. During this time, patience and fortitude werenoticeble characteristics in Mr. and Mrs. Mellen. She outlived her husband two years, 2 months, and 29 days. Their little daughter came to an untimely death by the report of a gun which was discharged very near her. She was immediately seized with convulsions, which continued at intervals until her death.

FOURTH GENERATION.

CHILDREN OF TIMOTHY MELLEN.

Timothy Mellen, born April 29, 1780. Lived in Holliston. Married Betsey Underwood, Nov. 25, 1802. Died Jan. 26, 1844.

Deborah Rockwood Mellen,	born	July 26, 1804.
Elizabeth Cutler "	"	Mar. 13, 1807.
Joanna "	"	Aug. 8, 1809.
Charlotte "	"	Dec. 25, 1812.
Harriet "	"	Dec. 4, 1815.
Miranda Pond "	"	Sept. 3, 1820.

Timothy Mellen died at his birth-place, aged fifty-four years, one month, and one day.

FIFTH GENERATION.

CHILDREN OF DEBORAH R. MELLEN.

DEBORAH R. MELLEN, born July 26, 1804. Lives in Holliston. Married Harrison Whiting, April 6, 1826.

George Addison Whiting,	born	Sept. 20, 1827.
Edwin Francis "	"	June 26, 1830.
Timothy Mellen "	"	Sept. 20, 1832.
Sydney Albert "	"	Oct. 12, 1835.
Georgianna "	"	Jan. 24, 1838.
Henry Harrison "	"	Jan. 29, 1841.
Charles Rockwood "	born	Ap. 26, 1844--died Aug. 11, 1844.
James Nelson "	born	Sept. 17th, 1845.

EDWIN F. WHITING.

EDWIN F. WHITING, born June 26, 1830. Lives in Holliston. Married Maria Payson, April 3, 1855.

FIFTH GENERATION.

CHILDREN OF ELIZABETH C. MELLEN.

ELIZABETH C. MELLEN, born March 13, 1807. Lives in Holliston. Married Benjamin Bridges, Oct., 1825.

Mary Elizabeth Bridges, born Sept. 29, 1826.
Benjamin Albert " " May, 1828.

Benjamin Bridges, died Nov. 18, 1828.

FOURTH GENERAT N.

ELIZABETH C. MELLEN.

ELIZABETH C. MELLEN, born March 13, 1807. Lives in Holliston. Married Newell Eames, Dec. 7, 1836. Mrs. Eames during the life time of her first husband resided in Milford. Soon after his death she went to New York city, where she remained until about the time of her second marriage. She now lives on the old homestead of her father, Timothy Mellen.

FIFTH GENERATION.

MARY E. BRIDGES.

MARY E. BRIDGES, born Sept. 29, 1826. Lives in Bellingham. Married Francis L. Wright, Oct. 5, 1854.

SIXTH GENERATION.

CHILDREN OF BENJAMIN A. BRIDGES.

BENJAMIN A. BRIDGES, born May, 1828. Lives in Holliston. Married Martha M. Johnson, Oct. 31, 1849.

Ida Jane Bridges,	born	Aug. 2, 1851.
Lizzie Frances "	"	Oct. 17, 1854.

FIFTH GENERATION.

CHILDREN OF JOANNA MELLEN.

JOANNA MELLEN, born Aug. 8, 1809. Lives in N. Y. City. Married Niles Eames, April 3, 1832.

Helen Maria Eames,	born	Mar. 10, 1833	—died Mar. 26, 1833.
George Henry "	"	Oct. 10, 1836.	
Niles Edgar "	"	May 16, 1843.	
Newell Francis "	"	April 4, 1845.	
Emma Adelia "	"	Dec. 5, 1850	—died Dec. 11, 1850.

CHILDREN OF CHARLOTTE MELLEN.

CHARLOTTE MELLEN, born Dec. 25, 1812. Lives in Hopkinton. Married Russell J. Burnap, Oct. 22, 1835.

Albion Gustavus Burnap,	born	July 25, 1837.
Charles Russell "	"	Aug. 15, 1842.

Mrs. Burnap has lived in Holliston, Medway, and Hopkinton. She is now at the latter place. Her husband is a thriving farmer Both are members of the Congregational Church in Hopkinton.

CHILD OF HARRIET MELLEN.

Harriet Mellen, born Dec. 4, 1815. Lives in Holliston. Married Charles Rockwood.

Adelia Maria Rockwood, born May 17, 1838.

Charles Rockwood died Feb. 16, 1842.

FOURTH GENERATION.

HARRIET M. ROCKWOOD.

Harriet M. Rockwood, born Dec. 4, 1815. Married Phineas K. Gage, June 23, 1852.

FIFTH GENERATION.

CHILD OF MIRANDA P. MELLEN.

Miranda P. Mellen, born Sept. 3, 1820. Lives in Holliston. Married Hamlet Barber, 1847.

Edna Perry Barber, born July 28, 1851.

Mrs. Barber was engaged for some years as teacher of public schools. During six successive years she was the superintendant of the Juvenile Sabbath School of the Orthodox Congregational Society in her native town. Much of the time, this school numbered more than fifty scholars, nearly all of whom were less than eight years of age. These little ones have manifested their regard for their teacher by constituting her a life member of the Massachusetts Sabbath School Society. May the good seed sown bring forth an abundant harvest.

FOURTH GENERATION.

CHILDREN OF ELIZABETH MELLEN.

ELIZABETH MELLEN, born April 29, 1780. Lived in Holliston. Married Martin Cutler, 1799. Died Oct. 28, 1805.

James Mellen Cutler, born Aug., 1800.
Simeon Cutler, born Aug. 20, 1802—died Dec. 28, 1802.
John Milton " " Feb. 9, 1804.

FIFTH GENERATION.

CHILDREN OF JAMES M. CUTLER.

JAMES M. CUTLER, born Aug., 1800. Lives in Holliston. Married Jemima Bullard, April 25, 1826.

Nelson James Cutler,	born July 9, 1827.
Henry Edmund "	" Sept. 26, 1831.
Albert Mellen "	" Oct. 23, 1833.
Ellen Jemima "	" Oct. 4, 1837.

NELSON JAMES CUTLER.

NELSON JAMES CUTLER, born July 9, 1827. Lives in Albany, N. Y. Married Sarah Fisher, July 9, 1855.

SIXTH GENERATION.

CHILD OF ALBERT M. CUTLER.

ALBERT M. CUTLER, born Oct. 23, 1833. Lives in Boston. Married Emma S. Dodd, 1854.

Thomas Cutler, born June 17, 1855.

FIFTH GENERATION.

CHILDREN OF JOHN M. CUTLER.

JOHN M. CUTLER, born Feb. 9, 1804. Lives in Holliston. Married Electa Burr, Oct. 21, 1830.

Eliza Ann Cutler,	born	Aug. 19, 1831.
Caroline Frances "	"	June 25, 1833—died Feb. 6, 1837.
Emma Burr "	"	July 20, 1835.
George Milton "	"	March 4, 1838—died Sept. 18, 1838.
Josephine "	"	Sept. 7, 1839.
Geo. Washington "	"	Jan. 7, 1842.
Caroline Mellen "	"	Nov. 13, 1844.
Jane Louisa "	"	Nov. 8, 1846.

SIXTH GENERATION.

CHILD OF ELIZA A. CUTLER.

ELIZA A. CUTLER, born Aug. 19, 1831. Lives in Holliston. Married Elbridge G. Whiting, Nov. 1, 1849.

Emma Louisa Whiting, born Sept. 18, 1852.

THIRD GENERATION.

CHILDREN OF RHODA ROCKWOOD,

AND SIXTH CHILD OF TIMOTHY ROCKWOOD, BORN IN 1727.

RHODA ROCKWOOD, was born Oct. 12, 1763. Lived in Holliston. Died March 23, 1822.

She had 5 children, 9 grand-children, and 2 great grand-children — of whom one child, 2 grand-children, and 2 great grand-children are now living.

Rhoda Rockwood, married Ezra Brown, Feb., 1782.

1. Amos Brown, born July 10, 1783—died Feb. 27, 1805.
2. Betsey " " March, 1785.
3. Ezra " " July 2, 1790.
4. Martin " " June 26, 1792—died Oct. 3, 1817.
5. Emily " " Sept. 14, 1800.

Rhoda Brown always lived in the town of her nativity — her place of residence after marriage, being but a short distance from her father's house. She was emphatically a child of affliction — was entirely blind during several years previous to her death. In view of her afflictions she was often left to repine at the good providence of God. Her husband was subject to hallucination of mind, which continned several months and resulted in insanity, and ultimately in death. He departed this life April 24, 1816.

Their first three children died of consumption, each of whom was 22 years old at the time of their death. Martin Brown survived his father only eighteen months. He also died of consumption, at the age of 25 years.

BETSEY BROWN.

Betsey Brown, born March, 1785. Lived in Holliston. Married Loammi Littlefield, June 22, 1807. Died Sept. 22, 1807.

FOURTH GENERATION.

CHILD OF EZRA BROWN.

Ezra Brown, born July 2, 1790. Lived in Holliston. Married Olive Adams, March, 1812. Died, 1812.

Betsey Brown, born 1812.

Olive Adams, wife of Ezra Brown, died Oct. 13, 1848.

FIFTH GENERATION.

CHILD OF BETSEY BROWN.

Betsey Brown, born in 1812. Lived in Holliston. Married S. G. Burnap, M. D., Nov. 8, 1832. Died Oct. 26, 1851.

Charles Brown Burnap born May 22, 1835—died Oct. 26, '51.

In the removal of Mrs. Burnap, society sustained the loss of one of its highly valued members. The zeal and fidelity with which she labored in the cause of Moral Reform, and in Maternal Associations, will long be remembered.

For some years previous to her death, she indulged the Christian hope, yet was ever fearful she might be deceived. During the last part of her life, however, she was enabled, by prayerful and earnest examination, to see every obstacle removed and to come off conqueror through Him that loved her with an everlasting love.

Not long after the death of Mrs. Burnap, this sorrow-stricken family was again called to mourn. Charles Brown Burnap, the only son of the above, survived his mother but few years. He had enjoyed feeble health for some time previous to his death. His life seemed to hang upon a slender thread, and he seemed early marked for the grave. He was cut down when just entering upon the threshhold of manhood. He died of consumption, Oct. 26, 1851, in the seventeenth year of his age.

That impressive scene, the celebration of the Lord's Supper a few days previous to his dying hour, evinced to the world that he regarded it an imperative duty, as well as a privilege, to join the church-militant on earth, ere he joined the church-triumphant in heaven.

It is sad and mournful, but a glorious sight, to see one so young as he step away, as it were, from the gentle declivity of time and behold with hope and joy the everlasting youth of heaven. There is an existence to which age never comes, and where there is measureless enjoyment which eternity will not sever!

FOURTH GENERATION.

CHILDREN OF EMILY BROWN.

EMILY BROWN, born Sept. 14, 1800. Lives in Holliston. Married Nicanor Pierce, March 2, 1823.

Harriet Rhoda Pierce,	born	Mar. 2, 1824—died Aug. 25, 1828.
Ezra Brown "	"	Oct. 2, 1825—died Sept. 1, 1828.
George Edwards "	"	Jan. 25, 1828—died Dec. 17, 1832.
Charles Henry "	"	Feb. 13, 1830—died Feb. 9, 1833.
Harriet Maria "	"	Oct. 14, 1832.
William Henry "	"	Nov. 14, 1834—died Sept. 25, 1842.
George Edwards "	"	June 2, 1836—died Oct. 1, 1842.

Nicanor Pierce, died of consumption Dec. 21, 1851.

Our relative, Mrs. Pierce, has been much in affliction. She has followed to the grave her father and mother, three brothers and an only sister; six children since August, 1828, and her husband in 1851. She has long enjoyed feeble health. May she find an inward peace the world cannot give, and may her last days be her best days.

FIFTH GENERATION.

CHILDREN OF AMOS BROWN.

Amos Brown, born April 14, 1819. Lives in Holliston. Married Mary Ann McLaughlin, 1843.

George Edwin Brown,	born Oct. 19, 1845.
Emily Maria "	" Dec. 6, 1847.

THIRD GENERATION.

CHILDREN OF LUCRETIA ROCKWOOD,

AND NINTH CHILD OF TIMOTHY ROCKWOOD, BORN IN 1727.

Lucretia Rockwood was born July 25, 1775. Lived in Plymouth, N. H. Died Jan. 29, 1817.

She had 7 children, 14 grand-children, and 2 great grand-children—of whom 5 children, 12 grand-children, and 1 great grand-child are now living.

Lucretia Rockwood, married Rev. Drury Fairbanks, May 25, 1800.

1. John Milton Fairbanks, born July 19, 1801.
2. Amanda " " March 8, 1803.
3. Drury " " May 27, 1805—died Dec.4, '10.
4. Mary " " March 31, 1807.
5. Timothy Rockwood " " April 15, 1809.
6. Lucretia Ann " " May 15, 1811.
7. Drury " " Aug. 7, 1813.

The following sketch of the life of our relative, by her husband, Rev. Drury Fairbanks, was published in connection with a sermon preached by him on the Sabbath following her death: —

"A Sketch of the Life of Mrs. Lucretia Fairbanks, consort of the Rev. Drury Fairbanks, who died at Plymouth, New Hampshire, Jan. 29, 1817, in the forty-second year of her life.

Mrs. Lucretia Fairbanks was born at Holliston, Mass., July 25, 1775. Her parents were professors of religion and exemplary in their lives. They instructed their children in the principles of religion, and were the means of forming impressions upon their minds which were lasting and of great use to them in their after lives. Lucretia, the subject of these memories, was afflicted from a child with various complaints, some of which followed her so long as she lived.

At about eight years of age her religious impressions commenced. She saw herself a sinner exposed to temporal death; and not only so, but to the wrath of an incensed God. What to do, and where to go for relief, she knew not; and still too diffident and proud to let her case be known. This state of mind, with some interruption, lasted for nearly a year. At length, as she advanced in age, these impressions left her. From this period of her life until she was about nineteen years old, nothing occurred that is very interesting to the Christian reader. Like other young people, she was for the most part thoughtless and inattentive to the great and momentous concerns of death. It should however be observed, that there were seasons in which she would be found bewailing her misspent life, and begging of God to have mercy on her soul.

At the age above mentioned she entered upon the work of school-keeping, and followed it for several years. In this new employment she had more time for reflection, and a better opportunity to learn what was in man. She now clearly saw that the fallen nature of Adam was somehow mysteriously entailed upon his unhappy offspring — that children, as soon as they were capable of moral action, discovered who their progenitor was.

These things, accompanied by the Spirit of God, led her again to look into her own condition. The result was, that she had not only a corrupt nature, but that she was a voluntary sinner—that she stood justly condemned by the holy law of God; and that no injustice would be done her should He frown her from his presence forever.

Thus this trembling sinner remained for months without hope, and sometimes in almost total despair. In this time she was favored with the faithful counsel of the late Rev. Timothy Dickinson, then minister of the place, who acted the part of a kind father and friend unto her. At length the scales of unbelief began to fall from her eyes. She now saw that although she was a condemned criminal, still a ransom had been provided; and Jesus, for the first time, appeared the chiefest among ten thousand, and the one altogether lovely. Her weary soul, which had for so long time been confined in the prison of sin, was set at liberty, and she found joy and peace in believing. Christ appeared a whole Saviour, yea, an Almighty Saviour, and she was willing to rest her eternal all upon his merits. But this disciple of the Redeemer was not permitted long to enjoy this happy frame. Clouds and darkness again overshadowed her, doubts and fears increased, and she was upon the point of giving up all for lost. Happily however for her this darkness was at length removed, and peace returned to her troubled mind. For some months after this she was tranquil, and took delight in reading God's word, and in waitiug upon him in his sanctuary. At length the following text occurred to her mind:—'*With the heart man believeth unto righteousness; and with the mouth confession is made unto salvation.*' 'This text,' she observed, 'whether applicable or inapplicable to my case, reminded me of my duty. I found that I had dishonored the cause of my Master by neglecting to confess him publicly. I resolved, though unworthy, to make the attempt, thinking that if I stayed away until I WAS worthy, I must stay away forever.'

About this time there were certain female Baptist professors, who were peculiarly intimate with her, and who were extremely anxious that she should come over to their communion. To the subject of baptism she had paid but little attention; and some of their arguments appeared plausible. This placed her in a perplexing situation; and she began to inquire of herself, 'What shall I do? One is for Paul, another for Apollos. Shall I take things for granted because my intimate friends say they are so? or shall I search for myself? The latter is the only proper alternative. I will take my Bible, and see what the Holy Ghost has to say upon this subject.' This resolution was not long delayed, but shortly executed. Her first object was to search into the ancient order of the Church. She looked at the covenant made with Abraham — found it to be everlastingly ordered in all things and sure. She noticed that in this covenant, the children of believers were included. It was then an object of importance with her whether Christ had done anything to dissolve this connection between parents and children. This she could not find. Her attention was then turned to the practice of the apostles and primitive Christians; and she there found that they proceeded in building churches upon the ground, that believing parents and their children were both embraced in this gracious covenant. The seal of this covenant she readily acknowledged was changed; but this by no means affected the right of children. They were the seed of the church, and as such, must have the seal placed upon them. After this careful examination of the subject, her doubts were removed and she united with the Congregational Church in Holliston.

At the age of twenty-five she was married to the Rev. Drury Fairbanks, pastor of the church in Plymouth, New Hampshire. On entering upon this relation she observed, 'that she was destitute of every qualification requisite to fill with propriety, this new relation. But,' continued she, 'if my heart is right I need not fear. God is able, and sometimes does make use of the feeblest saint to accomplish his everlasting purpose.'

The year that she moved to Plymouth, God was pleased to pour out his spirit upon that people, and a goodly number were called in. With this shower of divine grace she was much refreshed, and took a lively part in instructing and counselling those who were borne down with the weight of their sins. The substance of her advice to such was this, not to resist the Holy Spirit, but immediately to make an unconditional surrender of themselves to God. She was careful not to encourage them so long as they continued to give no evidence of a work of divine grace upon their hearts. It was her fixed opinion that persons under conviction grew no better. This she had learned by experience; for she often remarked, 'That until she was reconciled to God by faith in his Son, she grew more and more opposed to Him.'

For several years after this period she enjoyed but indifferent health, and a part of the time was unable to attend to the concerns of her family. Her constant difficulty was the nervous headache. This often rendered her exceedingly confused, and sometimes almost distracted. It also inclined her to melancholy. The dark side would often be turned towards her; and when this was the case, her hope would be gone, and the distress of her mind would exceed that of her body. In these unhappy hours she would often be led to wonder why such a wretch was continued to cumber the ground! 'Why does not God cut me off and send me to my own place? Surely, in so doing, no injustice would be done. I deserve to die, for I have long ago forfeited my existence. But stop; I am doing wrong. This is the language of impenitence and unbelief. It is all right. My condition is the best possible, all things considered, and I would not have it altered for the whole world.'

Such was the state of her mind, more or less, for several years. At one season in an almost hopeless condition; then rejoicing in hope, her soul fixed trusting in the Lord.

Christian reader, I think you cannot peruse the above lines without recalling to your mind the following scripture: Hebrew 12: 6, 'Whom the Lord loveth he chasteneth, and scourgeth every son whom he receiveth.' And again, 12: 8, 'If ye be without chastisement whereof all are partakers, then are ye bastards and not sons.'

Mrs. Fairbanks found that afflictions were salutary — they served as a purifying fire to purge out the dross from the pure gold.

For two or three years before her death, her mind was more even. She enjoyed the comforts of religion in a higher degree. In this time her mind was actively engaged in promoting the cause of the Redeemer, both at home and abroad. She had been a member of the Cent Society from its first establishment, and had taken great pains to call the attention of females to the subject. It was a common saying with her that a cent a week was but a mite, and if we give it freely, it may do incalculable good; but if it should do no good, we shall have the satisfaction of discharging our duty. The Foreign Missionary cause, the establishment of Indian Schools, Domestic Missions, the distribution of the Holy Scriptures gratuitously, and the translation of them into the various languages, together with the educating of hopefully pious men for the ministry, were objects which were near her heart. It was her constant prayer that God would smile on these attempts to reform an ignorant and wicked world. She was fully in the belief of the doctrine, that the more Christians did to promote the cause of Zion in foreign lands, the more they would be disposed to do at home. The year preceding her death she established a monthly meeting of the Church for prayer and religious inquiry; and in her dying moments expressed her desire that they might be continued.

Mrs. Fairbanks was much engaged in behalf of the Institution at Plainfield. She thought that females might afford considerable aid to indigent students who might repair thither for an education. She did not wish to dictate, but it occurred to her mind that persons of her sex might furnish considerable clothing without burdening themselves at all. She often remarked that she once thought that learning for a minister was of but little use, but she had lived long enough to see through the fatal delusion. 'What! must the mechanic, the physician and attorney serve for a course of years before they can be permitted to officiate publicly, and ministers of the gospel be suffered to go out and preach with but little, or no education at all? This is perverting the order of things and turning them upside down. No, let those who are designed for the gospel ministry be scribes well instructed into the kingdom, and let novices stay at home.' Such sentiments often fell from her lips; hence it is no wonder why she was so anxious that pious students should have help in order that they might be able hereafter to bring forth from the treasure of God's Word, things new and old.

Hitherto we have said nothing of this woman as a wife, a house-keeper and a mother. *As a wife*, she was tender, affectionate and faithful. *As a house-keeper*, she was a pattern for her sex in economy, and in directing in general her household concerns. She was ever busy in something. Her greatest fault was her over-anxiety for her family. This often led her to do more than her constitution could bear; and even in this, she appeared conscientious. Scarce ever could she be persuaded that she had done too much. *As a mother*, her affection for her children was peculiarly ardent. She was ever trying to do something to promote either their temporal or spiritual welfare. Those of them who were of sufficient age, will never forget her counsels, warnings and admonitions. The truth of that text — 'Train up a child in the way he should go, and when he is old he will not depart from it,' appeared to be constantly on her mind.

The closing scene of this woman was such as we might suppose. On the twenty-sixth of January, 1817, she was violently seized with the lung fever. In the outset her case appeared extremely doubtful; still fond hope seemed to whisper, she will recover. But alas! towards the close of the second day after she was taken, all hopes of her living were gone. At this time, though her pains were excrutiating, and respiration exceedingly difficult, yet her mind resembled an unclouded sky. All appeared to be peace within. She now called her children, six in number, and gave each in their turn a parting blessing. She told them they were sinners, and that they must in early life secure the favor of God. She reminded them of her former instruction, and earnestly entreated them not to forget them. To her husband she said,—'And you, my husband, the partner of my youth, go on in the work of the Lord—fight manfully the good fight of faith, and your reward shall be great in heaven.' After this, she requested prayers. The question was put to her,—'What are your desires?' She replied,—'That I may not be deceived; that I may have patience to wait my appointed time, and that I may have an easy passage into eternity.' After this time she said but little, for she was in a state of extreme debility.

The next morning, which was the morning of her death, it was perceived that she was going, her husband took her by the hand and said,—'If all is well with you, give me some token;' and she answered,—'It is well. The conflict is over; death is disarmed of its terrors, and I am ready to go.' In a few moments, without a struggle, she expired. Thus lived, and thus died this dear child of God, much beloved and much respected. Her trials, while on earth were great, and her conflicts were many; but she has gone, we trust, to that world where troubles never enter, and where she is perfectly happy in the full enjoyment of her God and Redeemer.

Go reader, go and live as she did, and your last end shall be like unto hers."

It is deemed not inappropriate in this connection, to insert here the following sketch of the life of Rev. Drury Fairbanks, the husband of Lucretia Rockwood. It is abridged from an Obituary, published soon after his death, in the *Vermont Chronicle*:—

"Died in Littleton, N. H., at his residence, January 11th, 1853, Rev. DRURY FAIRBANKS, in the eighty-first year of his age.

Mr. Fairbanks was born in Holliston, Mass., October 13th, 1772; graduated from Brown University in September, 1797; pursued theological studies during the next year under Dr. Emmons; was settled at Plymouth, N. H., March, 1800; was dismissed from that people in March, 1818; labored the next two years under the direction and patronage of the New Hampshire Home Missionary Society; was settled in Littleton, May, 1820; was dismissed in March, 1837, and retired to his farm where he lived till his death.

Mr. Fairbanks was one of the oldest ministers of the State at the time of his decease, and belonged to the class that has nearly passed away. The fifty-three years of his ministeriaı life saw many and great changes in the ministry and churches.

At Plymouth, a wide and important field of labor opened around him. Being one of the shire towns of the County and the seat of an academy, no ordinary effort was required to meet its wants. And then, as settled by the town, all the families of the town must be visited, not as now by callin for a quarter or half an hour, but by a regular afternoon and evening visit. He was subject, moreover, to frequent demands from the neighboring towns, in few of which were there ministers of his own order, to attend funerals, weddings, visit the sick, preach, lecture, and the like. Souls were gathered unto the fold of Christ and good seed sown, which, in after years, sprung up and bore fruit to the praise of God and the enlargement of the Church.

His two years of missionary life, were spent in the towns lying in the nighborhood of Plymouth, or at no great distance therefrom.

On going to Littleton, he settled in a still more destitute region than was that about Plymouth. The church here was small, and able to support him but part of the time, and the neighboring towns all around were entirely destitute. And extending his labors, as he did, to these towns, he made serious inroads upon his already impaired health.

Becoming anxious, for this reason, to resign the position he held, he took his dismission, as already stated, in March, 1837. From this time he preached only occasionally, and for the last few years of his life, not at all, his health not permitting."

To this historic sketch of the life of our deceased father in the ministry, we add the following extracts from the sermon preached at his funeral: —

"There was but little of incident in the life of our Rev. father and friend. It was a quiet, unobtrusive serving the will of God. The most he was accustomed to say, was, that he had *tried* to do some good; that he had *tried* to preach the Gospel of Christ, though he had made but poor work of it, compared with the merits of the cause. And as it was in respect to his serving the will of God in efforts for the good of his fellow-creatures, so it was in respect to his serving the will of God in efforts for his personal sanctification.

In his last sickness, the day before his death, he spoke with the best utterance he could command, of the great wickedness of the heart, repeating the declaration of Jeremiah: 'The heart is deceitful above all things and desperately wicked,' and saying that is superlative enough, and yet it is none too strong to express the truth in my own case. At the same time he trusted in Jesus, and accepting him as all his plea and all his hope, he felt an inward peace that made him ready and anxious to go.

He has not only gone from us in a good old age and full of years, but after a service which makes all recollections pleasant, and associates him with the skies. He was here as watching for souls and receiving souls for his hire. He was here as loving the church, even to his last day. His age, his office, his deeds, his spirit, entitle him to warm remembrance.

Paitiently toiling on for seventeen years, doing what he could for the religious and moral prosperity of the place, as connected with the growth of the church and living to see it in its present aspect, he should, and will live in our recollections; the tear will start from our eyes as we think of him as gone. At the same time, as he has gone, after having secured the will of God and having lived as he did, we feel to sing in the words already employed,

'Methinks from Earth I see him rise,
Angels cougratulate his lot,
And shout him welcome to the skies.' "

FOURTH GENERATION.

CHILDREN OF JOHN M. FAIRBANKS.

John M. Fairbanks, born July 19, 1801. Lives in Coventry, Vt. Married Mehitable Knapp, March 20, 1827.

Laura Fairbanks.	born June 29, 1829.
Horace K. Fairbanks,	" April 19, 1843.

A somewhat eventful chapter of incidents in the life of John M. Fairbanks, came to pass at the time he first came to Holliston, in the spring of 1823. Small and single acts in life are often good indices of the whole character, and so we here make note of his first tour from Littleton, N. H., to Holliston, Mass. He was conveyed in a private carriage from Littleton, N. H., (his residence) to the White Mountain Notch. After walking from thence twenty-five miles, he took the Stage for Concord, N. H. The Stage broke down twice before reaching its destination, and in Concord street gave way again. To use his own language at the time, "the posts and beams began to fall out, and eight Green Mountain boys, his companions, picked them up, and marched single file to the tavern and pawned them for something to drink!" He went the remainder of his journey on foot. The road was hilly, wet and muddy. He reached Holliston on the fourth day from Concord, stiff-jointed, sore footed, and literally jaded. His predicament being not much unlike that of Benjamin Franklin when he first entered the streets of Philadelphia, except he had not in his possession the blessing of Franklin's loaves.

He spent about a year in Holliston, got wofully poisoned, and was otherwise much afflicted. Soon after leaving Holliston he went to reside in Portland, Me. In 1825 he settled in Coventry, a small township in the northern part of Vermont. At that time that portion of the country was a vast wilderness, almost uninhabited save by wild beasts. Our relative here witnessed the revolutions, and experienced the hardships and privations incident to the first settlers of a new country. The first summer he passed in this, his new home, he came near being killed by the falling of timber upon his head, causing a rupture of the skull. His residence at this time was fifty miles from any Bank, and almost from any money! The traffic was *barter trade*, in grain, sugar and ashes. *The Collector of School taxes* was wont to call on his few scattered fellow citizens with a grain bag and measure in hand, soliciting of them a half bushel, a peck, or two quarts of grain as the case might be. *School Teachers were paid in store goods. The miuister even came under the barter system.* The salary usually paid him was four hundred dollars per annum, one half money, and the other half meat, stock and grain. Traffic by such exchanges is obsolete there now, and the country is beautifully diversified with works of art. But vast forests are still there; their majestic trees seem to vie with each other in their upward and strong growth, yet all are harmonious in carrolling the grandeur, power, and omnipotence of the Great Supreme. A change has effected our relative also, religiously as well as physically. Once his hope of salvation was in good works, now in faith on a crucified Saviour. He has courage and perseverance. He is a sterling, common sense man, who knows how to apply it practically. He seems to be the happy recipient of the confidence and esteem of the community. "His head is silvered o'er with age," which he regards as a solemn admonition of his early dissolution.

CHILDREN OF AMANDA FAIRBANKS.

AMANDA FAIRBANKS, born March 8, 1803. Lives in St. Johnsbury, Vt. Married Samuel G. Brackett, Jan. 1, 1827.

Mary Ann Brackett,	born Jan. 30, 1828.
Samuel Augustus "	" Dec., 1829.
Elmore Fairbanks "	" May 26, 1839.

Mrs. Amanda Brackett is a Deacon's wife. We trust that the injunction by the inspired Timothy is being portrayed in her life, "Even so must their wives be grave, not slanderers, sober, faithful in all things."

We delight to record, that Dea. and Mrs. Brackett are of those, who we trust, are instruments of good, inasmuch as they are the parents of one who has consecrated herself to God in the work of a *Foreign Missionary.*

FIFTH GENERATION.

CHILDREN OF MARY ANN BRACKETT.

Mary Ann Brackett, born Jan. 30, 1828. Married Dr. Fayette Jewett, Feb. 17, 1853, Missionary in Tocat, Asia Minor.

Mary Amelia Jewett, born July 16, 1854—died July 26, 1854.
Henry Martin " born July 8, 1855.

Mrs. Jewett early devoted herself to her Saviour, and her life evinces that this devotion was sincere, and that her self-consecration to the work of a Missionary was the dictate of her love to the cause of Christ. Her husband was ordained a few weeks previous to their departure. They sailed from Boston, March, 1853. For nearly two years after this they were verily strangers in a strange land, but now have found a most delightful, though heathen home, in Tocat, Asia Minor, the place of their choice and their labors.

In the society of Rev. J. H. Van Lennep and wife, they labor under many pleasant and encouraging circumstances, with the hope of an extended influence and usefulness. They have experienced many vicissitudes and trials, which have chequered the pathway of their early missionary life. In view of it relatives and friends here would gladly convey to them their encouragement and sympathy in such lines as the following:

Christian Sister, shrink not thou,
God will be thy trust, thy stay;
He the cloud to shade thy brow,
He the light to guide thy way.

A small mound, covered with wild flowers, on that far off and heathen land, is precious to us, for beneath it lies interred a little one — Christ has said "of such is the Kingdom of Heaven." At the judgment of the great day little Mary will rise, with her relatives in this land, triumphant from the grave, though her mouldering remains may be away from ours full a thousand leagues.

FOURTH GENERATION.

CHILDREN OF MARY FAIRBANKS.

MARY FAIRBANKS, born March 31, 1807. Lived in St. Johsbury, Vt. Married John Bacon, Oct. 21, 1828. Died Sept. 28, 1840.

Nancy Jane Bacon, born July 20, 1833.
Edwin B. " born April 28, 1838—died June 18, 1842

CHILDREN OF TIMOTHY R. FAIRBANKS.

TIMOTHY R. FAIRBANKS, born April 15. 1809. Lives in St. Johnsbury, Vt. Married Katharine Stevens, Sept. 22, 1840.

Wm. Rockwood Fairbanks, born Dec. 1, 1841.
Emma Katharine, " born July 22, 1845—died Dec. 22, '45.
George Stevens " " Nov. 29, 1847.
Katharine Emma " " Dec. 3, 1853.

Timothy Rockwood Fairbanks is rightly named, for his character partakes largely of the originality of the parent stock. We hope the name, character, and race identified with it, does not, and will not prove a counterfeit in any relatives, antecedents, or succedents!

Timothy Rockwood Fairbanks commenced mercantile life in the town of Waterford, Vt., in the spring of

1833, and was there engaged in his chosen employment about eleven years. In 1845 he took an agency for the celebrated Scale Company of Messrs. E. F. Fairbanks & Co., of St. Johnsbury. Here has been his home about seven years. Since taking this agency he has spent a large portion of his time in the New England States and New York. He has travelled through the Canadas, New Brunswick, Nova Scotia, New Jersey, Delaware, Pennsylvania, Maryland, and in parts of Ohio, Illinois, Indiana, Michigan, and Wisconsin. Though a travelling agent in toto, he has spent a portion of each year, quietly and calmly at home, enjoying the sweets of domestic bliss. Within the last two years his peregrinations have been less; so that now, we are happy to say to any one of his relatives, or others who may call upon him, that they will find him *at home.*

CHILDREN OF LUCRETIA A. FAIRBANKS.

Lucretia A. Fairbanks, born May 15, 1811. Lives in West Newport, Vt. Married Joseph A. Ide, Jan. 24, 1838.

George Henry Ide,	born Jan. 21, 1839.
Edward Milo "	" April 30, 1841.

Mrs. Ide is a "*farmer's wife*," and decidedly prompt in all her domestic duties. She it is that "spinneth wool and flax, and worketh willingly with her hands."

CHILD OF DRURY FAIRBANKS.

Drury Fairbanks, born Aug. 7, 1813. Lives in Philadelphia. Married Susannah C. Owens, Jan. 26, 1845.

Drury Rockwood Fairbanks, born July 14, 1851.

Drury Fairbanks was a stammerer, but has been untiring in his efforts to subdue it. He has labored to overcome the defect with a perseverance akin to the illustrious Grecian Orator, and has been alike successful. No traces of this difficulty are now perceptible He is a mechanic. Residence No. 928, Coutes-street.

THIRD GENERATION.

CHILDREN OF ANNA ROCKWOOD,

AND TENTH CHILD OF TIMOTHY ROCKWOOD, BORN IN 1727.

Anna Rockwood was born June 14, 1777. Lived in Hopkinton. Died Dec. 21, 1843.

She had 6 children, 25 grand-children, and 5 great grand-children — of whom 2 children, 16 grand-children and 4 great grand-children are now living.

Anna Rockwood, married Sampson Bridges, 1795.

1. Luther Rockwood Bridges, born July 20, 1800.
2. Roxanna Bridges, born Feb. 20, 1803.
3. Joanna " " March 28, 1806.
4. Willard " " July 11, 1809—died Sept. 10, 1827.
5. Amos Brown " " May 26, 1811.
6. Dexter " " April 6, 1813.

Mrs. Bridges became a resident of Hopkinton in 1779. Her acquaintances there were limited in number, but marked by strong attachment. She was not only a *sympathizer with the sick*, but emphatically a helper in very deed. *She was an unostentatious woman.* All her useful and benevolent acts were performed from a high sense of duty. Often while thus engaged, she felt deeply her ill desert, and would frequently ejaculate it in mournful and sorrowful expression. "*I am nobody; I am nothing; I am good for nothing*," were so often repeated by her, that they became her peculiar and chosen household words. When trouble, sickness, or distress came into her neighborhood, there she was found; and when *her* last and dying hour came, she had the presence and sympathy of large numbers of friends, to whose necessities in her health she had so often and fondly ministered.

As a house-keeper she was wise in calculation, shrewd in management, and one who executed much, with comparatively little ado. *She was a peace-maker*, ever "leaving alone contention before it be meddled with."

A disease of the head terminated her lifetime, which numbered sixty-six years, six months, and seven days. Her husband died April 6, 1846, thus surviving his wife two years, three months and fifteen days. The ages of their four children who have died, were 18, 52, 37, and 33 years respectively.

FOURTH GENERATION.

CHILDREN OF LUTHER R. BRIDGES.

Luther R. Bridges, born July 20, 1800. Lived in Hopkinton. Married Hannah Stearns, 1822. Died April 28, 1852.

Elizabeth Ann Bridges, born April 17, 1823.
Daniel Thurber " " Oct. 15, 1827.
Hannah Thayer " " Oct. 22, 1829.
Sampson " " June 6, 1833.
Kesiah Goddard " " Apr. 29, 1835—died Sep. 15, 1835.
Emeline Stearns " " Dec. 9, 1837.
Angeline " " June 3, 1839—died Aug. 28, 1839.
Mary " " Jan. 17, 1842—died May 7, 1842.
Alvira " " Dec. 9, 1843—June 25, 1844.

Luther R. Bridges died of consumption, and was buried at the Central Cemetery in Hopkinton. His surviving children reside at home with their mother. Daniel Thurber Bridges, his oldest son, has ever manifested a kind and commendable regard for his widowed mother and sisters. By his fidelity, he has also gained the entire confidence of his employers, having the oversight of a large manufacturing establishment in Hopkinton.

FIFTH GENERATION.

CHILD OF ELIZABLTH A. BRIDGES.

Elizabeth A. Bridges, born April 17, 1823. Lived in Hopkinton. Married Richard Gammage, jr., Nov. 28, 1839. Died Aug. 31, 1844.

Emma Elizabeth Gammage, born Aug. 9, 1844—died Sept. 26, 1844.

FOURTH GENERATION.

CHILDREN OF ROXANNA BRIDGES.

ROXANNA BRIDGES, born Feb. 20, 1803. Lives in Hollis, N. H. Married Richard Patch, 1829.

Amos Bowers	Patch,	born Aug., 1830.
Harriet Ann	"	" Nov. 1831.
Ellen Maria	"	" May, 1833.
Mary Jane	"	" March 23, 1835.
Jerry M.	"	" July 12, 1836—died Oct. 1, 1841.

AMOS B. PATCH.

AMOS B. PATCH, born Aug., 1830. Lives in Union City, Indiana. Married Eliza A. Hunter, August 17, 1853.

FIFTH GENERATION.

CHILDREN OF HARRIET A. PATCH.

HARRIET A. PATCH, born Nov., 1831. Lives in Hollis, N. H. Married John C. Smith, May 30, 1850.

Imogien Harriet	Smith,	born May 26, 1851.
Herbert John	"	" Sept. 18, 1853.

CHILD OF ELLEN M. PATCH.

Ellen M. Patch, born May, 1833. Lives in Hollis, N. H. Married William R. Sargent, Oct. 16, 1847.

Warner Bridges Sargent, born Nov. 1, 1848.

Ellen M. Sargent was divorced from her husband by a decree of the Court, about the year 1851.

FOURTH GENERATION.

ELLEN M. SARGENT.

Ellen M. Sargent, born May, 1833. Lives in Hollis, N. H. Married Lorenzo Quaid, Jan. 24, 1855.

FIFTH GENERATION.

CHILD OF MARY J. PATCH.

Mary J. Patch, born March 23, 1835. Lives in Hollis. Married Noah Dow, April 11, 1854.

Melvin Noah Dow, born June 22, 1855.

FOURTH GENERATION.

CHILDREN OF JOANNA BRIDGES.

Joanna Bridges, born March 28, 1806. Lived in Hollis, N. H. Married Silas S. Wheeler, Dec. 22, 1835. Died very suddenly, July 9, 1843.

Silas Bainbridge Wheeler, born Sept. 8, 1837.
Maria Jane " born Dec. 29, 1839—died July 5, 1853.
Eliza Ann " " Mar. 22, 1841—died Sep. 7, 1855.
Fidelia Augusta " " June 22, 1843.

CHILDREN OF AMOS B. BRIDGES.

Amos B. Bridges, born May 26, 1811. Lived in Hopkinton. Married Frances W. Heald, March 26, 1834. Died March 23, 1844.

Lucretia Rockwood Bridges, born May 31, 1839.
Amos Willard " " March 13, 1843.

CHILDREN OF DEXTER BRIDGES.

Dexter Bridges, born April 6, 1813. Lives in Hopkinton. Married Rhoda Cady, Jan. 6, 1841.

Mary Elizabeth Bridges,	born	Dec. 7, 1841.
Anna Augusta "	"	Sept. 10, 1843.
Adeline Hannahetta "	"	March 14, 1845.
Wilber Clinton "	"	March 12, 1854.

Dexter Bridges owns and occupies the old homestead of his father. The old family mansion still stands, as in years long past, and with it the great willow tree at the corner, the acqueduct, the old cider mill, and many other antique and time-honored surroundings. We know of few old residences now in existence, around which are clustered so many dear associations of the past. "Woodman spare that tree," we say. May no ruthless hand tear down the old house. Let all remain as we now see it, and may all of good that has been said or done within those old walls be hallowed in our memories.

THIRD GENERATION.

CHILDREN OF LUTHER ROCKWOOD,

AND ELEVENTH CHILD OF TIMOTHY ROCKWOOD, BORN IN 1727.

Luther Rockwood was born Jan. 7, 1780. Lives in Holliston,

He has had 9 children and 16 grand-children; of whom 5 children, and 5 grand-children are now living.

Luther Rockwood, married Ruth Perry, Dec. 27, 1801.

1. Mariam Rockwood, born Aug. 2, 1803—died Mar. 10, '14.
2. Albert Perry " " June 9, 1805.

Ruth P. wife of Luther Rockwood, died Aug. 31, 1805.

Luther Rockwood, married Ruth Temple, Dec. 23, 1806.

3. Elbridge Luther Rockwood, born Oct. 3, 1808–died Aug. 7, 1813.
4. Mary Ann Rockwood, born June 13, 1810–died Aug. 5, '13.
5. Thomas Temple, " " June 5, 1812.
6. Eveline " " Sept. 14, 1814— " Feb. 17, 1819.
7. Ruth " " June 5, 1816.
8. Elsie Lucretia " " Dec. 13, 1819.
9. Elbridge Luther " " Nov. 24, 1824.

Ruth Temple Rockwood, died Oct. 11, 1855, aged 75 years. She joined the Congregational Church in Holliston in 1817.

The following lines were suggested by some of her last words, which were, "*I want to go home*:"

"I WANT TO GO HOME."

"I know that thou hast gone to the home of thy rest,
Then why should my soul be so sad?
I know that thou hast gone where the weary are blest"
And thine eye looks up and is glad.

In thy far away dwelling in heaven above
I believe thou hast visions of me—
How much in my memory of favor and love
Familiarly whisper of thee!

I have a conviction that thy presence is nigh,
When my prospects are shrouded in gloom,
Or whenever I look for blessings on high
Or when weeping over thy tomb.

Mine eye is so dark for I know not how soon
Ere again it may gaze upon thine;
"But my heart has revealings of thee and thy home
In many a token and sign."

By Hope it is revealed, as stars are by night,
That ere long to thy rest I may come;
And Faith, like a rainbow, breaks on my sight
And shows me thy kindred and home.

Luther Rockwood is the only surviving child of the Timothy Rockwood whose genealogy is the subject of these pages. He received from his father the homestead estate, situated about a mile west of Holliston Central Village.

Luther Rockwood has served his fellow-citizens in various town and military offices. We think it can be said, that, in sickness and trouble his friends and neighbors have found in him a valuable and abiding counsellor. He has been one of the largest owners of real estate in town; and its management has made his life one of earnest, active and laborious effort. Not always successful in his business, we think he has been found in the path of duty and honorable exertion.

There are incidents peculiar to every family which it is often well to remember, for every event in the affairs of men bears the impress of an all-controlling and superintending Providence, and we may learn therefrom the wisest lessons of life.

In the summer of 1813, three children of Luther Rockwood were at the same time prostrated by the same disease, and no hope entertained of their recovery. But two of them, however, were marked for a premature death. The other, Thomas Temple, still survives, a monument of God's sparing mercy.

Luther Rockwood, like his father before him, is a Congregationalist of the old Puritan stamp. He has been much in affliction. He has followed to the grave two wives, four children, and eleven grand-children.

Since the death of his last wife, with whom he lived almost fifty years, he sadly feels his loneliness.

May that religion which he has so long professed, sustain and support him through his remaining days, and make them calm, peaceful and happy.

FOURTH GENERATION.

CHILDREN OF ALBERT P. ROCKWOOD.

ALBERT P. ROCKWOOD, born June 9, 1805. Lives in Great Salt Lake City, Utah Territory. Married Nancy Haven, April 3, 1827.

Elizabeth Perry Rockwood, born Dec. 28, 1827—died Sept. 22, 1838, in Quincy, Ill.

Ellen Ackland Rockwood, born March 23, 1829.

Albert Haven " " Sept. 29, 1831—died Sept. 8, 1838, in Quincy, Ill.

Meriam Rockwood, born Feb. 16, 1834—died Mar. 28, 1834.

Mary Ann " " Feb. 16, 1834—died April 5, 1834.

Albert Nelson " " Feb. 19, 1841—died July 18, 1843.

An event untoward, unlooked for and incomprehensible, came to pass in this family in the spring of 1838. That religious humbug of Joe Smith and others, called Mormanism, was embraced by many in Holliston during that year, and among the number were our relatives, Albert P. and Nancy H. Rockwood.

From that day to this, they have defended the notions, followed the teachings, and endured the toils and hardships of this peculiar and deluded sect. He was with them in their pilgrimage from Missouri to Illinois; from thence back to the frontier settlements of Missouri again, and to Great Salt Lake City. He was one of the small party of pioneers who made a tour of exploration from Council Bluffs, Mo., to Utah Territory, in 1847.

He is of sanguine temperament, and *has untiring perseverance and indomitable courage.*

Previous to 1838, temperance, anti-slavery, military tactics and medicine were the prominent subjects that engaged his attention.

Very few, in these days of progress, ingenuity and thrilling adventure, have lived a more chequered and toilsome life than Albert Perry Rockwood.

CHILD OF THOMAS T. ROCKWOOD.

THOMAS T. ROCKWOOD, born June 5, 1812. Lives in Norton. Married Evelina Leonard, Feb. 10, 1841.

Charles Hodges Rockwood, born March 10, 1842.

We will venture here to notice one foot-print in the sands of time in the history of Thomas T. Rockwood. It was enstamped in Feb., 1838, and is described in the following *metre*, most of it written about the time of the occurrence, but some of it afterwards!

THE BROKEN LEG.

As I was riding in the stage
  From Worcester on to Keene,
There was a most unlooked affair
  Befel the coach and team.

Before we rode two-thirds our way
  The stage became upset,
And we were thrown around the road
  Into the mud and wet.

The driver he was womewhat hurt —
  Alas! I broke my leg —
He hallooed out for nearest help,
  While I was forced to beg.

Then soon we rode to Abbott's Inn,*
  And here I had it set,
And now I first began to think
  I 'd pain "to sell or let."

I had a most distressing time
  The first few days I 's sick —
My appetite was almost gone,
  My fever called for drink.

But ere two weeks were fully past
  I rode in safety home;
And when we got some crutches made
  I longed on them to roam.

Nor were my wishes wholly lost,
  I hobbled round the town,
And thus I gained my wonted health,
  A boon of kindness shown.

* In Holden.

CHILDREN OF RUTH ROCKWOOD.

Ruth Rockwood, born June 5, 1816. Lives in Holliston. Married Eli H. Warren, Aug. 9, 1840.

Ellen Lucretia Warren,	born	Sep. 6, 1841—died June 15, 1847.
George Harrison "	"	Sep. 3, 1843—died Aug. 16, 1851.
Emma Maria "	"	Apr. 8, 1846—died Aug. 23, 1851.
Ella Maria "	"	April 30, 1853.

Eli H. Warren died of consumption, May. 30, 1853.

Ellen Lucretia Warren died of the same disease when a little less than six years of age. She was an interesting child. The following lines composed for the occasion, were sung at her funeral by eight little misses, who were nearly her own age:

Tune — Warning Bell.

Farewell, dear one, thy pains are o'er,
Thy transient race with us is run;
How short thy hours laid up in store,
How soon thy earthly errand done.

And could we not protract thy stay
To fill our thousand fancied joys?
Ah no! t'is God who takes away—
'T is He our fondest hope destroys.

Our loss, O God! we deeply feel
And humbly beg thee to appear;
O let thy smiles our sorrows heal,
O let us feel thy presence near.

When we the lonely spot shall tread
  To weep around dear Ellen's grave,
Be thus the thought our feelings shed:
  He takes but what He kindly gave.

CHILDREN OF ELBRIDGE L. ROCKWOOD.

ELBRIDGE L. ROCKWOOD, born Nov. 24, 1824. Lives in Holliston. Married Elizabeth Phipps, 1846.

Wilber Norman Rockwood, born May 9, 1847.
Evelyn Marilla " born Dec. 10, 1848—died June 24, '52.
Herbert Luther " " Oct. 12, 1850—died Sep. 14, 1852.
Eva Elizabeth " " June 16, 1853—died Aug. 3, 1854.
Edwin Elbridge " " March 16, 1855.

An incident of note we here chronicle, occurred in the spring of 1833. Our relative, Elbridge Luther Rockwood, was seized with the malignant small pox. That he should recover, was regarded by the old and skilful family physician as little less than a miracle.

There were at that time thirteen occupants in the old family mansion, who were shut out from all society during seven long weeks. Many of the medical profession from abroad came to see the sick and learn relative to this malady. During its prevalence, the wants of the family were supplied at *seemingly* great hazard to the health and safety of the surrounding neighborhood. All were shut in, the roads fenced up, and all regular outward communication cut off!

There was a place prominent and particular, where the family was permitted to make known its wants to those in waiting. This was at the top of the "Powder-House Hill," so called. Here communications, written and verbal, were responded to from the valley below; and the various articles needed, allowed and called for, were in due time set down at the thither side of the fence full half a mile from the infected district. The house "with all its appurtenances thereunto belonging," was considered infected by this dread malady.

After the restoration of the sick, the house, with the various paraphernalia, including a heterogeneous assortment of odd and antique commodities in the old garret, were ordered to be cleaned by thorough washing, and the process completed by smoking in fumes of brimstone. The place of purification was a small shop hard by the house. Our worthy town officials for the time being, to make things all right, "on a set day" entered and examined the premises and pronounced them clean and safe, every whit.

Thus ended the history of the small pox in Holliston in 1833. "A consummation most devoutly wished" by the whole town.

The Lithograph at the commencement of this volume, represents THE HOUSE OF TIMOTHY ROCKWOOD. It was built in 1720, by some persons now unknown.

He purchased it in 1750 when it became his residence, and remained so until his death in 1806. It then passed into the possession of his youngest son, Luther. It was demolished in 1850, having remained in possession of "The Rockwood Family" just one hundred years.

Tradition says that 20 persons have died in this house, since 1750, namely: Sarah Rockwood, the second wife of Samuel, the father of our progenitor. She came here from her home, three miles on foot, and died very suddenly while shelling beans, aged 96. Also, Timothy Rockwood, his 4 wives, 5 of his children and 4 of his grand-children; Ruth P., the first wife of Luther Rockwood, and 4 others not relatives.

The following lines were written by one who remembers the house, not only as his "Grand-father's home," but the home of his own childhood:

" Our grand-father's home, old home dearest to me, —
Its serpentine brook, and balm-gilead tree,
The horse-block and corn-house each side of the way, —
I remember them well, as if 't were to-day.

At the ends of the house, two ash trees were seen,
And lilacs all round it in purple and green;
The willow and hop-vine that grew near the brook,
The bridge we fished from and the lilies we took;

The little brown pear-tree, the apples to bake,
The wood-colored fence, and the leather-hinged gates,
The great wood-pile with milk-pans and trays, —
Were highly prized blessings in those olden days.

A spring from the pasture, its sweets to distil,
Came in aqueduct logs cut out from 'The Hill,'
It run to the house in a jubilant tide,
While a branch at the barn the cattle supplied.

But nothing I loved so, nor shall love for aye,
As *the house we lived in* in grand-father's day,
So quaint and old-fashioned, so anciently rude,
The family mansion in quiet it stood.

I remember the outlines presented to view, —
One story in front, in the rear it had two,
Then its low slanting roof, with moss tufted o'er,
Its brick-colored walls and batten front door.

Reflection is active, it hastens aback
To scenes of the past in this oft-beaten track —
To hopes and to pleasures, to joy and to woe,
The old house has witnessed in times long ago.

Brave manhood has been there and lived out its days,
The infant has nestled and boys had their plays,
The vows of the wedded there often were said; —
How may, alas, have gone down to the dead!

The aged have lived there, and nervously told
Of his fights with the bear and Indian of old,
How toilsome his care 'twixt the war and his sheep,
Purchasing blessings for his children to keep.

We often remember, nor would we we forget,
The joyous out-gushings of relatives met;
The Catechism heard, when the pastor was there,
The dear old Bible and the family prayer.

Yes, often does fancy most vividly trace
The acts and the scenes of this time-honored place,
And the faces of those, who, dwelling herein,
Life's battles have fought, its blessings to win.

How painful to see in the short distant past
The relative leave it who lived in it last,
To quit its old rooms, its wide chambers and door,
To dwell 'neath its roof and its shadow no more!

Old house of our father! thou art gone to decay,
We leave thee in sorrow and sadness for aye,
'T is thus *we* must leave when a few days are o'er
'The house that we live in' to dwell here no more.

Norton, Sept., 1855.

[The manuscript containing the record of this family was unfortunately mislaid. Its proper place is next after page 28.]

FIFTH GENERATION.

CHILDREN OF EMILY A. ROCKWOOD.

Emily A. Rockwood, born March 30, 1808. Lives in Ashland. Married Geo. W. Jones, Jan. 1, 1834.

George Edward Jones, born Oct. 11, 1834.
Sarah Albee " " July 14, 1836.
Theodore B. " " Apr. 11, 1838—died Mar. 16, 1839.
Theodore " " May 8, 1840.
Charles Rockwood " " Feb. 6, 1843.
Harley " " Apr. 19, 1846—died Apr. 26, 1846.
Harvey " " " " " " " May 8, 1846
Helen M. " " July 1, 1847.
Emily " " Aug. 8, 1849.

Mrs. Jones, from early childhood until eighteen years of age, lived with her grand-parents in Holliston. Since her marriage, she has lived in Keesville, N. Y.; Grafton, Framingham, and Ashland, Mass.

INDEX.

PART I.---GENEOLOGICAL.

FIRST GENERATION.

SECOND GENERATION.

INDEX.

PART II. --- HISTORICAL.

ERRATA.

PAGE 11th, 8th line from the top—read 1727 for 1724.

" 12th, 12th line from the bottom—read Anna for Ann.

" 24th, 14th line from the top—read, before leaving home, after he uttered.

" 35th, 9th line from the bottom—read born for died, and after 1836 read died Dec. 1836.

" 61st, 5th line from the top—read 1853 for 1854.

" 63rd, 8th line from the top—read first for third.

" 81st, 3rd line from the top—read saw for has seen.

" 93rd, 2nd line from the bottom—read about 1839 for 1835.

" 97th, 7th line from the top—read sixty-four for fifty-four.

" 98th, 9th line from the top—read Bridges for Mellen.

" 105th, last line—read May 6, 1842.

" 121st, 6th line from the top—read rolls for loaves.

" 128th, 7th line from the bottom—read 1795 for 1779.

www.ingramcontent.com/pod-product-compliance
Lightning Source LLC
LaVergne TN
LVHW021407110826
845150LV00007B/1820

* 9 7 8 1 4 2 5 5 1 1 9 1 3 *